# A Dream for South Central

## THE AUTOBIOGRAPHY OF AN AFRO-AMERICANIZED KOREAN CHRISTIAN MINISTER

BY

## WARREN W. LEE

In gratitude, humility, and hope, with unspeakable love,
I dedicate this book to my wife Susan,
my children Jonathan and Rebecca,
and my mother Mrs. Whamok Lee.

Copyright © 1993 by Warren Lee. All rights reserved.
No part of this work may be reproduced or transmitted
in any form or by any means electric or mechanical,
including photocopying and recording, or by any
information storage or retrieval system, except as may
be expressly permitted by the 1976 Copyright Act
or in writing by the Author.

Printed in the U.S.A.

Library of Congress Catalog Card Number: 93-080837

ISBN: 0-9639920-0-7

*Cover design: Sasaki Stuff*
*Body text: Adobe Garamond with Helvetica Black heads*

# Table of Contents

Foreword .................................................................. IV

Preface ................................................................... VII

CHAPTER 1 ............................................................. 1
   What's God Got to Do with It?

CHAPTER 2 ........................................................... 11
   Lust Is Blond

CHAPTER 3 ........................................................... 31
   Save Me a Seat

CHAPTER 4 ........................................................... 49
   Gratitude, Humility, and Hope

CHAPTER 5 ........................................................... 71
   Divide and Conquer

CHAPTER 6 ........................................................... 87
   I Believe in the Resurrection

Epilogue ................................................................ 105

# Foreword

One day, out of nowhere, Warren Wonkyeng Lee appeared at a meeting of the senior high fellowship group of the Westminster Presbyterian Church in Los Angeles. None of us knew where he came from or how he got there. None of us knew why he was there, this short bespectacled Korean dude, most recently from Princeton Theological Seminary, whatever that was. He drove a white, stripped-down, manual transmission (gear on the steering column, not on the floor!) Ford. It had an AM radio and a heater. Period. When that car expired — mercifully, I thought — he bought another one exactly like it. He absolutely never exceeded the speed limit. He was never in a hurry. He wore clothes of no particular style or note whatsoever, anything in his wardrobe could be worn with anything else.

Clothes meant nothing to him, cars meant nothing to him. He lived in what I remember as a one-room house, and that designation is generous. It was nearly invisible from the street, and I do not remember exactly where it was, so infrequently was I there. To say he lived there is generous as well; he slept there. But he lived more deeply in our hearts with each passing day.

Warren changed our lives completely. If I cannot say this for the entire congregation, and I want to, I can say it with confidence for our youth group and with complete, joyful confidence for myself. We were teenagers in the midst of the ferment of the sixties: civil rights, black power, war and peace, counter-culture challenges to settled roles for men and women, changing attitudes toward sex, the increased use of "recreational" drugs.

In our group we would talk about subjects we either could not or would not discuss in other places, home especially. We read and talked about *The Autobiography of Malcolm X*, about relationships and sexuality, racism, faith, war, and peace. We visited white and black groups from churches vastly different from our own. Warren took us camping at Big Bear, Lake Arrowhead, and Forest Home, a clash of religious perspectives and experiences if ever there was one. We grew our "Afros" or "Bushes", wore our bell bottoms, army fatigues, or miniskirts; marched and demonstrated and sat-in at sit-ins. We boldly participated in those critical times in both the life of our nation and our own lives. Warren did not make our decisions for us, he was our wise mentor, our pastor and friend.

While Warren may not have owned a stereo record player, he did own a guitar. He sang and played. After meetings on Sunday nights he would take us to Shaky's Pizza Parlor on LaCienega Boulevard. We would sing loud, bouncy, Christian songs none of us would have had the inclination or the nerve to sing otherwise. At Christmas we would go caroling together and gather at someone's house to laugh and sing. With Warren everybody could sing, whether they thought so or not. Affirming one's identity and gaining acceptance in the social world of high school are brutal and mystifying processes. Warren created for us a safe place to explore openly what we thought and felt about our world, each other, and our private selves.

Warren's energy was limitless, his passion for life infectious, his steady baritone voice irresistible. Yes, he was a great basketball player. He had eyes in the back of his head and an unerring jump shot. And yes, he is a great preacher. He has the courage to say even the most difficult words of truth, as you will soon discover. But what Warren did best then and now is love. He gives himself completely to life, as he did to the people of Westminster, to our youth group, and to me.

In the pages that follow Warren tells his story. Not enough of it by my account; I believe there is more he could tell us, and I trust he will when he is ready. His life to this point is an American story: peculiar in its details, universal in its appeal, and resonant with life in multicultural America in the last days of this remarkable century. We've gone from walking the earth to floating in space, from pen and paper to laptops and microchips, from home remedies to the brink of genetic engineering. If these changes suggest giant strides into the future there is equally good evidence that humanity has been treading in place. Old divisions and fresh hate in every generation: Catholics and Protestants in Ireland, Serbs and Croats in Bosnia, Arabs and Jews in Palestine.

In our land, neighborhoods continue to change as wave upon wave of immigrants make the United States home. A glorious quilt of shifting patterns, shapes, and colors is being created. It is beautiful. Let us say that and celebrate. But there is more to say. Where new cloth is set next to and sometimes over old cloth, where binding stitches loosen, where new seams are sewn in fabric unfamiliar to the pattern, in those places tension exists. Will the new material work gracefully with the old to enhance the whole? Will it hold together or tear under the stress? Beautiful as it may look from a distance, when we come close to the places where new meets old, can we still talk of beauty and grace?

Warren writes because in his experiences he has found those places where the many places of our national guilt converge. He reconciles the elements of his identity and experience into a coherent life. His story brings a wind of hope to the uneasy co-existence of blacks and Koreans in an America which is only beginning to understand its present and future as a multilingual, multicultural reflection of the world. This wind of hope is for all of us, and it originates in the gospel of Jesus Christ. It is in the pages of the New Testament, the life of Jesus, to which Warren turns for understanding of how we are to live together. Let him speak to you as he has to me and to so many others.

Michael E. Livingston

Princeton, New Jersey

November 19, 1993

# Preface

My favorite scene from the movie *Superman I* has teenager Clark Kent engaged in a heart to heart conversation with kindly Pa Kent played by Glenn Ford. In the previous scene, Clark has been humiliated in front of his would-be girlfriend, Lana Lang, by the star player on the local Smallville High School football team on which Clark is the water boy. Chagrined and frustrated, Clark says to his father, "That cocky prima donna gets me so mad. He's not that great and I know I'm better than him. Why I could score a touchdown every time I get my hands on the ball." Knowingly and lovingly, Pa Kent replies, "Son, I don't know exactly what your purpose in life is, but one thing's for sure, it's not to score touchdowns." Of course, several scenes later and what every fan of Superman knows, his reason for being is revealed: to fight for truth, justice, and the American way.

Like young Clark Kent, for many years I didn't know what my exact purpose in life was either, and at times this fact also left me chagrined and frustrated. All that has changed now. At age 51 I have a clear vision of what I was meant to do, vocationally speaking, and this book is an expression and result of this conviction. It is no accident that I am Korean, that I was raised in South Central Los Angeles, that from the year 1949 on I attended public elementary, junior high, and high schools that were predominantly black, that I was an Associate Pastor for seven years at the largest African American Presbyterian church in the western United States in the late 60's and early 70's, that I consider myself a theological and spiritual disciple of Martin Luther King, Jr., that I lived through the 1965 Watts Riots, and that I am here proclaiming the gospel of Korean and African American solidarity in the aftermath of the Rodney King verdict-incited spring, 1992 Los Angeles social upheaval.

My purpose in life is not to fight for truth, justice, and the American way, it is to serve as an agent of reconciliation between my two communities of origin, heritage, participation, and identity. I do not pretend to have any special or easy answer to the problem of African American-Korean American relations, but I do believe my autobiographical journey and ideas on the subject can help promote greater understanding of both groups toward each other and in the process contribute something positive to the redeeming and healing of our society as a whole. Whether or not I succeed in this effort is up to the reader to decide but I offer what follows with this hope and in this spirit.

I want to take this opportunity to thank San Francisco Theological Seminary for granting me a sabbatical leave to write this book. I am especially grateful to my colleague in Advanced Pastoral Studies, Walt Davis, for his inspiration, encouragment, and willingness to assume the lion's share of my work responsibilities. Also, I want to thank Pat Perry and Norma Lannert for taking on an extra load because of my absence in the APS office. Finally, let me express appreciation for the many others whose names do not appear in these pages, but without whom I could not have gotten the job done. They know who they are and I am grateful to each one.

CHAPTER 1

# What's God Got to Do with It?

The title of this chapter is taken from Tina Turner's hit song of several years ago, "What's Love Got to Do with It? Answer for what *God* has to do with it: everything. From my earliest memories as a child, I believed in God. Of course, the image I had in mind was that of some sort of super Santa Claus figure who could do just about anything He pleased. It should go without saying that I no longer believe that God is an older white male person, even though I continue to have faith in a personal deity who is kind, loving, and has blessed us human beings with gifts both in the past and will continue to do so in the future.

Be that as it may, the point I want to make here is that however dimly and vaguely, I have always had a sense that God was watching over me and that this God had given me life for a reason. Like the earlier alluded to young Clark Kent, when I was a teenager, I wanted that purpose to be, not scoring touchdowns but scoring field goals on the hardwood and making Magic Johnson-type assists as a point guard in the NBA. As many boys growing up in the ghetto, for a time basketball was my life and I actually dreamed of playing in college and becoming a professional athlete. Some of my fondest memories of growing up in South Central L.A. are the "gym rat" days. Especially during my years at Manual Arts High School from 1956 to 1959, my buddies and I would make the rounds from places like Jefferson High School, Denker Playground, Sportsmen's Park, Normandie Playground, and Exposition Park. At 5'5" I couldn't sky like Spud Webb but I could go behind my back like Bob Cousy and pass the ball like Guy Rodgers. To this day I love and follow the game, and would still probably come to blows with anyone who tries to tell me that Michael Jordan is the greatest player who ever lived and not Kareem Abdul-Jabbar. When I was a student at Princeton Theological Seminary from 1963 to 1966, I almost killed a white guy who is now a prominent pastor of a large church in the east for trying to tell me Bill Bradley was better than Elgin Baylor. Get serious. I still love the Lakers and hate the Celtics. I lived through every dribble and missed Frank Selvy shot the 8 times my team lost to Boston in the NBA Finals, so I'm not shuckin' and jivin' when I say the second happiest day of my life was June 9, 1985 when the Lakers finally beat the Celtics at the Boston Garden to claim their first of two World Championships against their old nemesis. To be sure, let me make it perfectly clear that the single happiest day of my life was January 19, 1980 when at the age of 38 I took Susan Leong to be my wedded wife in the backyard of my oldest sister's house in Rolling Hills Estates.

Wait a minute the reader is asking just about now. What's God got to do with the Los Angeles Lakers? Answer: everything. The God who created the majestic beauty and absolute perfection of a Kareem Abdul-Jabbar sky hook shot from the right baseline of the second game of that aforementioned momentous 1985 NBA Championship Series, is the same One who brought my parents, Suntu (father) and Whamok (mother) Lee together to become husband and wife in their culturally prearranged marriage in Pyong Yang, (North) Korea in 1916, and whose love for each other in turn gave me birth on January 5, 1942 in an area of Los Angeles about one mile due north of Virgil Junior High School. In 1949 when I was 7 years old, our family consisting of my parents, three sisters (Kay, Sally, and June with a fourth sister, Aikyung, still living in Korea at the time) moved to South Central L.A. one block north of Jefferson Boulevard on Vermont Avenue. It is there my saga, culminating in the writing of this book, began.

I cannot possibly express in words fully and adequately what the experience of growing up in South Central L.A. means to me. I can only testify that I am convinced that it was through the grace and providence of God that it happened. It was part of the master plan for my life that the Creator who calls each of us by name and who knows even the number of hairs we have on our head, consecrated me before I was formed in my mother's womb from the foundation of the world, for this to be so. Accordingly, I hereby affirm and claim my black cultural heritage and black spiritual identity as a divinely ordained privilege and unspeakably wonderful gift from God. My response from the depths of my heart and soul for this fact can only be "Thank you, Jesus."

Lest I give the impression that I am some pie-in-the-sky uncritical fundamentalist looking at my past through rose-colored glasses, let me quickly add that the reason my family moved to precisely where it did at the time is that it was about the only place in the entire city where Koreans could buy homes because of restrictive covenants. As such, this area was the geographic center of that era's Korean American community of Los Angeles, which even then contained the largest concentration of Koreans living in the continental United States. To be sure, the Korean Presbyterian Church, founded in 1906, was located there a few houses west of Budlong Avenue at 1374 West Jefferson Boulevard. I was baptized as an infant in this congregation and learned how to sing "Jesus loves the little children, all the children of the world; red and yellow, black and white, they are precious in his sight; Jesus loves the little children of the world" from my Sunday School teachers in that setting.

Having moved to 3022 ½ South Vermont Avenue in 1949 where my father owned a small jewelry shop in front of our house located on a busy thoroughfare, I began the second grade at Vermont Avenue Elementary School. Our family was poor but my childhood could not have been happier emotionally and socially. When I asked my father for a penny, he gave me a nickel. When I asked him for a nickel, he gave me a dime. When I asked him for a dime, he gave me a quarter. My mother, who at the age of 47 plus had given birth to my younger sister June in 1946, had begun to work at a downtown sewing factory sweatshop in the garment district. She was to toil there until the age of 65 and so qualify for the Social Security pension she is receiving to this day. My great mama turned 95 on October 15, 1993.

When I look back on my elementary school years, the main reason I appreciate and cherish it so much now is that it was truly and wondrously multi-racial and multi-cultural. There were significant numbers of blacks, Hispanics, Asians, and whites (who had not fled to the suburbs yet). My personal experience convinces me of the value of integrated public schools, with a key being that there is a sufficient critical mass of each ethnic group present so that no individual of any particular group is a token member. I have seen the psychic damage done to one's self-esteem when people have grown up in situations where they were isolated without the support of their ethnic community. One reason I consider myself normally neurotic and not hopelessly psychotic in terms of psychological identity, given the brutal realities of our racist American society, is that through God's grace I was fortunate enough to belong to a peer group of boys and girls just like myself at the Korean Presbyterian Church. Had this been otherwise, growing up in that crucially important formative childhood period would have been destructive and unbearable. Speaking of my generation of Korean peers, who were born and raised in this country, ethnic sociologists have dubbed us the First Wave. This is to distinguish us from the Korean immigrants who have come to America since the immigration law was changed in 1965 permitting Asians to enter the U.S.A. in the same number as Europeans.

Let me just describe a few individuals from my grammar school days to give the reader a flavor for the multi-cultural richness that was a joy to behold and why now I can only finally explain as a precious gift from God. The names themselves say it all. First, when African Americans come to mind, there was Annie Tolliver, Carmelita Brown, Melvin Johnson, and yes, Michael Jackson. Annie and I are close friends to this day, and even as I write these words she and I are the prime movers in putting a committee together to plan the 35th Year Reunion of the Zirconian senior class of 1959 from Manual Arts High School. Carmelita was one tough customer but she liked me and protected me from the other second graders who might do me harm. Melvin Johnson was the baddest dude I had ever met to that point in my life, but he too took a shine to me. Michael Jackson even bore some physical resemblance to his megastar namesake of today, but he was much more like Billy Dee Williams in style and suaveness.

When white folks come to mind, there were WASP-types like Jerry Side, Larry Harvey, and Aaron Clark. There were Jewish guys named Paul Jacobs and Walter Polsky although at the time I didn't know the difference between a Jew and Gentile. There was Ruth

Linford, the All-American Lana Lang cheerleader, Bobby Dye, who went on to become a great basketball player and successful coach, and a little blond-haired with pigtails girl who transferred into Vermont Avenue Elementary School around the fourth grade named Jutah Vahar. I mention Jutah because she came from a country I had never heard of until I met her: Estonia. Enough said.

When Hispanics come to mind, there was Mario Mendoza, Gordie Morales, and Art Avilez. Mario brought the most incredible lunches to school consisting of beef-bean burritos. Gordie, who actually went to St. Agnes Catholic School right across the street from Vermont Avenue, as did come-to-think-of-it, Michael Jackson, was the best all-around athlete in the neighborhood. Gordie was a nickname. His actual name was Henry, but he was a chubby baby so he was called Gordie (gordo meaning fat in Spanish). Art Avilez lived next door and I never had to buy a pair of baseball cleats because he gave me his, which I wore through high school as the best fielding but worst hitting second baseman in the history of Manual Arts Junior Varsity baseball.

When Asians come to mind, there was Howard Tsujimura, Kay Ebihara, Gary Matsuno, and Donald Imai. Howard played shortstop like Phil Rizzuto and I emulated the way he drove to the hoop. Kay Ebihara had tremendous artistic talent and later married an equally creative white guy she met at Manual Arts named Chris Holly. How I inwardly envied Gary Matsuno and Donald Imai. They had Rawlings mitts and rode Schwinn bikes. They were also in the Cub Scouts which I yearned to join but couldn't because the cost of $12 for the blue uniform and yellow scarf was simply too much money. Howard, Kay, Gary, and Donald were all Japanese Americans. There weren't as many Chinese kids at school or in the neighborhood because they lived further east beyond what is now the Harbor Freeway where their ethnic enclave was located. Nevertheless, one Chinese family, the Yees, lived right down the block from us where, sure enough, they ran a small Chinese food take-out restaurant.

When I entered Foshay Junior High School in the fall of 1953, I weighed 53 pounds dripping wet. I remember this very clearly because in the P.E. (Physical Education) class in the seventh grade, it was the first time I had my exponents taken. At my adult height of 5'5" and

133 pounds, I am a small man but as a young child throughout elementary and junior high school, I was superduper tiny. My 8 year old son Jonathan, who is not a particularly big kid, already weighs over 60 pounds and he's just in the third grade. No wonder I saw myself the way I did and developed feelings of inferiority and inadequacy. However, I now consider even this fact as ultimately a gift from God and a part of the divine master plan for my life because it made me try my hardest athletically. In addition to having a positive ripple effect in other areas of my personality, I became as about as good a 5'5" basketball player as ever put on a pair of size 7 black low-cut Converse sneakers. Be that as it may, Spud Webb and Mugsy Bogues have definitely caused me to reevaluate my self-proclaimed assessment of where I stand in the pantheon of great hoopsters under 5'7". I now consider myself only the third greatest of all time!

Foshay Junior High School was predominantly African American, perhaps 10% Asian, 3% Hispanic, and 2% other. I felt sorry for the whites because the few of them there were regularly harassed. Remember the earlier point I made about critical mass. This applies to white folks too because no one should have to go to school in an atmosphere of fear and intimidation. I would still argue, however, that this experience in the long run is not anywhere near as damaging psychically on Caucasians as on racial minorities, because the society as a whole through all the means at its disposal — textbooks, newspapers, movies, television, etc. — wages a daily all-consuming assault on the self-esteem of its black, brown, red, and yellow citizens. T.V., especially, is pernicious for non-white children because they watch so much of it and its influence is so powerful and pervasive. Not too long ago, my 6 year old daughter Rebecca, even though she attends a neighborhood public elementary school which is genuinely multi-racial critical mass-wise in terms of Asian, black, and white constituency, came home and out-of-the-blue announced that she wanted to have blond hair. Both my wife Susan and I had had bad days at work that particular day, fighting the powers that be. We almost packed our bags on the spot to catch the next plane to Hawaii. We vacation there every year because we enjoy the feeling of being in the majority. To be sure, Hawaii, underneath its tourist-trap image is no multi-racial paradise, but for Asian Americans at least it's a great place to raise children. We have the luxury there of feeling about ourselves the way white people feel about themselves on the mainland. Maybe Susan should have explored that job possibility teaching Early Childhood Education at the University of Hawaii that came up a while back. After all, I've been contacted and encouraged by friends in Honolulu willing to run interference for me to apply for pastorates over there. Hmm...

Getting back to Foshay Junior High and 1955, that was the year I first heard the name of one who would decisively shape my consciousness on racial matters and give voice to my highest ideals and deepest yearnings about the human condition: Martin Luther King, Jr. He burst on the national scene at that time as the leader of the Montgomery Bus Boycott when courageous Rosa Parks refused to give up her seat to a white passenger on her way home from work. That event, of course, marked the beginning of the Civil Rights Movement, which I followed religiously in the newspapers and media as a teenager, and participated in actively as an adult in ensuing years. In the person of Dr. King, I found a man and a cause to believe in. As he once said, "Unless you find something worth dying for, you're not fit to live." From 1955 to 1968 when he was assassinated by James Earl Ray, he incarnated my hopes for racial justice, in particular, and for a better world, in general. When he died, a part of me died with him. However, the assassin's bullet which took Dr. King's life may have killed the dreamer, but it couldn't kill the dream. In 1993 25 years after he was gunned down, I am more committed than ever to carry on his vision of the oneness of humanity. Red and yellow, black and white, we are all precious in God's sight.

Something else took place during my junior high school years which I think the reader might find interesting, although I don't put it in the "What's God got to do with it" category. But it really did happen, folks. Honest. I was a child television star. When I was 13 years old, representatives from the weekly 10:00 Sunday night T.V. dramatic series, *The Loretta Young Show*, visited the Korean Presbyterian Church looking for some real live Koreans. They had come to cast people for parts in an upcoming episode based on a story coming out of the Korean War (1950-1953). Since I had always been an extrovert and a ham of sorts (two attributes I now also consider personal gifts from God), I was chosen to play a major speaking role that was integral to the plot. Thus began a part-time professional acting career that lasted about three years.

Remember how small I said I was at that age. Well, at 13 I could have passed for 7 or 8. This is why I can identify with what Steven Spielberg does in his movies. All those incredible kids he gets to act in his pictures, from *E.T.* to *Jurassic Park*, are probably 5 to 6 years older than the roles they play on screen. My part was basically always the same: cute little street smart Korean or other Asian refugee type boy who allowed the white hero, in my case stars such as Rock Hudson and Cesar Romero, or white heroine, like Loretta Young, Celeste Holm, and Gail Storm, to save me from some tragic fate. In addition to the *Loretta Young Show*, I appeared on such memorable programs as Cesar Romero's *Passport to Danger*, Gail Storm's *Old Susanna*, and a Rock Hudson full feature film, *Battle Hymn*, in which my scene did not make the editor's cut. I made the then astronomical sum of $100 a day during that time, and maybe God did have something to do with it because my parents saved all the money I made from these roles to finance my college and seminary education.

The money was good, but I didn't really enjoy acting. Intuitively I knew that God had not put me on this earth to win Oscars or Emmys. Scoring touchdowns, as much as I liked football was not it, although I had not yet abandoned the idea that leading the fastbreak was not my main purpose in life. At the age of 16 at a church high school summer youth conference at a Forest Home, a half hour drive from Redlands, California in the San Bernadino Mountains, elevation 5,280 feet, exactly one mile closer to heaven, I publicly declared at week's end during testimony time in Victory Circle, that I felt called by God to preach the gospel of Jesus Christ and to become a minister in the church. Alas, my true purpose in life, as far as what profession to pursue is concerned, thus determining what my education would be after graduating from high school, had been revealed to me. It is no accident that my announcement took place in rather melodramatic adolescent fashion in front of perhaps 500 fellow conferees, 99 and $^{44}/_{100}$ % white except for my peer group of 9 jive-talkin', signifyin', and otherwise Afro-Americanized guys from the Korean Presbyterian Church, who were trying to hit on all the surfer girls.

Meanwhile back at the ranch, I want to talk about my experience at Manual Arts High School. The three years from 1956 to 1959 were incredibly happy, gratifying, and full. Just the thought of them brings a smile to my face and joy to my heart. This is not to say that these "good old days" were any better racism-wise and prevailing social conditions-wise in South Central L.A. as a whole than they are today. To be sure, one important objective difference is that drugs and guns were not the truly demonic scourge they are now, but chronic urban problems such as poverty, unemployment, crime, police brutality, and domestic violence plagued the community in the 50's as they do in the 90's. There is no other way to understand the 1965 Watts Riots.

It was at Manual Arts that my esteem for black people and the identification with black culture, begun at age 7 in the second grade, blossomed into a full blown love affair and spiritual symbiosis that would last a lifetime to this day. Of course by birth I am not a person of African American descent, but by adoption, as surely as by this means Jonathan and Rebecca came to be Susan's and my son and daughter, as surely as there is but one "birth" son of God, even Jesus Christ our Lord, and all the people of the earth throughout time and history are God's children by adoption, I embrace and celebrate blackness as my own, not as a birthright but by adoption. This does not mean I am any less proud and accepting of my Korean cultural heritage and identity, because I am. However, it was not until much later as an adult that I came to a full awareness and appreciation of my biological roots.

I do not think it will be difficult for the reader to understand my feelings about Manual Arts and how blackness came to enter my soul for time and eternity once I describe what it was like for me there. In a student body that was perhaps 90% African American, I was given opportunities to express and maximize the full range of my gifts and abilities. I studied under competent and dedicated teachers of different racial backgrounds who took a personal interest in me. I sang in the best boy's glee club in the history of humankind, when we performed our special finale rendition of "Onward Christian Soldiers," brought the house down every time. I was the song leader for the after school *Youth for Christ* club and became a member of the highest on-campus boy's service organization, the Knights. I was Captain of both the "C" and "B" basketball team and was given a spot on the Varsity in my junior year when we went to the annual All-City tournament. I was elected President of the Lettermen's Society, and the reason this is so special is that this happened to a 5'3 ½" Korean in a predominantly black inner city high school well known throughout Los Angeles for its great athletic tradition. The final and most significant honor bestowed upon me by my African American peers is that I was elected President of the Senior "A" Class of Summer 1959, the mighty Zirconians. This is where I exercised my gift for public speaking and other leadership skills that I didn't even know I had.

It was originally in the black community, then, that my needs for recognition and achievement in the crucial identity-forming adolescent years were fulfilled. All people, young and old, require a nurturing and supportive social environment in which to actualize their full human potential. Not only was I nurtured and supported, I received praise and acclaim that exceeded my wildest expectations. Black people, in general, and black individuals, in particular, beginning with Annie Tolliver and Carmelita Brown in the second grade throughout the course of my life, have been gracious and kind to me. They have affirmed and loved me, and through their affirmation and love I have come to know the goodness and grace of God. In turn, one of the primary characteristics of my understanding of blackness and why it is so incredibly beautiful, is that race doesn't matter. Not at least for black people. They will recognize you, in the words of Dr. King, not for "the color of your skin, but the content of your character."

Let me come to the close of chapter 1 by referring to a one-liner from a speech I once made in my senior year. It says it all in summing up what growing up in South Central L.A. means to me and what God has to do with it. If anyone reads this book who was there that day in that student body assembly in 1959, I bet my bottom dollar they remember a little Asian dude who-thought-he-was-black and could make people laugh say, "You may eat beans, greens, or rice, we are all Manualites." Thank you, Jesus, and Amen.

CHAPTER 2

# Lust Is Blond

I have entitled this chapter "Lust Is Blond," which just as easily could have been called "In Search of Wendy WASP," to cover my ongoing autobiographical journey during college at UCLA (1959-1963) and my seminary years in Princeton, New Jersey (1963-1966). The reasons will become clear soon enough. It was my high "I wish I were white" period, although I didn't realize it at the time. I don't think any of us colored folk — red and yellow, black and brown — really ever do. As the case may be, this is certainly how I would characterize a major psychological struggle I was having with myself during these years, and all I can say is, it almost destroyed me. Ultimately and finally, were it not for God, I think it would have. Suicide perhaps, at worst, and at best, an adult life filled with frustration, anger, depression, and despair because of choices made on the basis of mistaken identity. Our racist American society will never let us forget that we are not white. It will always do everything in its awesome and unrelenting power to keep us "in our place." It will never, like Manual Arts High School, judge us by the content of our character but the color of our skin. This is where I agree with Derrick Bell's piercing analysis about the permanence of racism in American culture in his latest book, *Faces at the Bottom of the Well* (New York: BasicBooks, 1992). This, for my money, and Cornel West's most recent book, *Race Matters* (Boston: Beacon Press, 1993) should be required reading for every man, woman, and child in America.

The line "Lust is blond" comes from a well known psychotherapist in the San Francisco Bay Area named Marty Klein. I once heard him say, "Love is blind but lust is blond." It is a humorous way of making a profound point about the manner in which sexuality is understood, packaged, and merchandised in American culture. It has a particularly devastating effect on people of color for the end result of it is that it makes us reject ourselves and want to be white. I am not trying to speak here for all racial minority women and men. Their experience and understanding may be quite different from mine, but I do think that if they are honest and objective, especially the men, they will be able to see themselves in my struggles with this issue. I am going to describe and critically analyze how this "Lust is blond" syndrome worked on me during my college and seminary years, consciously and unconsciously, affecting every area of my life. On this score, I agree with Sigmund Freud and psychoanalytic theory that sex and aggression lie at the base of all human behavior like a "boiling cauldron." Unless we recognize and deal with these two realities, we will never be able to understand and accept ourselves truly and fully from a psychological and emotional standpoint.

I want to return to a discussion of the call I heard to enter the ministry at the age of 16 at the Forest Home Christian Conference Center, elevation 5,280 feet exactly one mile closer to heaven. I believe it illustrates the way the "Lust is blond" syndrome operated on me. First, it created within me a burning, yearning, face-pressed-up-against-the-glass sexual and romantic desire for white women, especially blond-haired, blue-eyed ones. Second, however, this desire could never be consummated because of the color of my skin — psychoanalytically speaking, my genitals would have been severed (as was literally done to countless numbers of black men in the history of this nation). Third, I then sublimated this forbidden desire and accompanying repressed anger into something that was socially acceptable, even praiseworthy, to the surfer girls, in particular, and to the larger white majority community gathered there at the time, in general, i.e., the announcement that God had tapped me on the shoulder earlier in the week and called me into the ministry. Fourth, this action served the purpose of providing me with a very specific and concrete answer to the problem of my adolescent youth identity crisis, regardless of whether or not it was healthy or unhealthy, good or bad.

Looking back in retrospect, I don't think I would have received the call to ministry the way it in fact happened at Forest Home if I had not gone to that particular kind of summer youth conference with the

"Lust is blond" syndrome operating on me as it was. The four-fold process I just described would not have worked the same in a Korean or African American setting. First, the racist society as a whole and my immediate social environment were not creating impossible to fulfill forbidden desire toward Asian and black girls. Second, therefore, no need existed to sublimate repressed feelings to socially acceptable channels of behavior. There were no societal impediments, and punishments like symbolic castration awaiting me, if I admitted and acted upon my romantic and sexual impulses toward non-white girls. Only my personal sense of inferiority and idiosyncratic inhibitions, both of which were highly developed, held me back with those "of my own kind."

    I am almost sure now that I would not have decided to become a minister during my adolescent years were it not for my mountain-top experience at Forest Home. This is why I believe it was part of the divine master plan for my life that this vocational decision took place exactly when, where, and how it did, psychological dynamics and racial considerations notwithstanding. It really was God's voice that spoke to me one mile closer to heaven calling me to preach the gospel of Jesus Christ. It is this call which has sustained me in the ministry for the past 27 years and given me the spiritual strength to persevere as an ordained pastor in a denomination, the Presbyterian Church (USA), which, for all that's good about it, is as racist as the society to which it belongs. There have been a number of times during the past two and a half plus decades that I have felt like giving up on the church and doing something else to earn a living. Psychologically and emotionally, I have been beaten down and ready to call it quits. It is in these moments that that same voice I heard as a surfer girl-obsessed 16 year old, has spoken to me in a still small way and said, "Let not your heart be troubled, neither let it be afraid, I have overcome the world." I may have been down, but I was not out. There was some One in my corner who would not give up on me and had the knack of always saying just the right thing at the right time. I'm sure there'll be more times in the future when I'll have to pick myself up again from the canvass of life and come out swinging. I realize championship fights no longer go 15 rounds, so in my 12 round endurance test as a Presbyterian minister, I'd say I just heard the bell for round 9.

Staying with the boxing image for the moment, from an overall standpoint my four years at UCLA (1959-1963) were spent mostly down on the canvass. It was not a happy time for me. I had been Mr. Everything at my beloved Manual Arts High School in South Central L.A. At UCLA in West L.A., I was Mr. Nobody and felt like IBM #26,999 out of a student body of 27,000. This was my first time living, moving, and having my being in a predominantly white environment on a permanent basis. Until then the most sustained contact I had had with white people in the flesh, where they were in the majority, was one week at summer church youth conferences. No doubt my college years would have been very different had I had my way with things. During my senior year at high school, I dreamed of attending a small college in the Midwest where I could play varsity basketball and become a B.M.O.C. One of the sons of our Pastor at the Korean Presbyterian Church, George Kim, whom I worshiped, had attended Wooster College in Ohio and had done just that. My parents would not allow me to go away to school, primarily for financial reasons, so it was off to UCLA I went where I commuted by car to Westwood every day for four years.

Because of the "Lust is blond" syndrome, I think now that I would have ended up marrying Wendy WASP were I to have gone to that small church-related college of my dreams. Who knows, maybe I would have been a small college All-American and in view of my former childhood acting career, abandoned my ministerial aspirations, returned to 3022 ½ South Vermont Avenue as an all-conquering hero and become Chick Hearn's color commentator on L.A. Laker broadcasts. Hmm... Meanwhile back at the ranch, the reason I believe it is highly likely I would have married a white girl in the scenario I just painted is, first, all Presbyterian colleges of the kind I am describing were certainly then, and probably still are, 99 and $^{44}/_{100}$% white. Second, no matter how short and ugly I was, in view of my wizardry on the hardwood playing in front of those nothing-else-to-do-on-Saturday-nights-in-Wooster packed field house crowds, I think I would have managed to hit successfully on a 5'5" or under Lana Lang look-a-like. Even though neither her nor my parents would have approved, being away from home and the support we would have received from student peers on campus, would have given us the courage to tie the knot. Third, and probably most important, there was the "boiling cauldron" factor. What I mean by this is that given the fact that the way I had been raised and the commonly held religious values of that era did not allow sexual intercourse before marriage, I think the underlying power of libidinal drives would have forced Wendy WASP and me to the altar.

In point of fact, I know a number of racial minority guys of my vintage who followed this pattern. Some of them are still married but many have gone through a divorce as a result of a mid-life identity crisis. After 20 years or so into marriage with a cooled down "boiling cauldron," as their children are leaving the nest, these men begin to raise serious questions about the meaning of their life. They ask themselves, who am I and what do I want to do with the rest of my life? Most of the time these individuals genuinely love their spouses and have tremendous guilt about inflicting emotional harm on their wives because of what they are experiencing. As a result of this struggle of the soul, some end up returning to their ethnic family and community of origin, even remarrying the second time around with "one of their own kind." Others decide that what they have built through the years is too much to give up. Accordingly, they make the decision to stay "until death do they part" with the mother of their daughters and sons.

God knows us better than we know ourselves. So do our parents, most of the time. Looking back, I am glad now that I didn't get what I wanted by attending a small mid-western college but instead went to UCLA. I didn't make All-American but I did make it to the All-U Intramural Finals in my junior year and our Korean Presbyterian Church basketball team took the All-City Church Athletic Association Championship two consecutive years. I also played at the highest level in the Nisei (Japanese American) League which allowed each team up to three non-Japanese Asians on its roster. Hmm... Marrying Wendy WASP, I suppose, would not have been the end of the world. Had I done so, however, I'm pretty sure I would have been like the first group of racial minority guys I just described, who ended up returning to their family and community of origin after going through a mid-life identity crisis. My mid-life transition has been tough enough as it is. I just thank God that I don't have to live with the fact of having put Wendy

WASP through pain and anguish she never asked for 20 years down the road from when she first saw me throwing behind-the-back passes at the Wooster College Field House.

At this point I want to discuss an incident that happened to me in my freshman year at UCLA which is one of those archetypal moments that define this period of my autobiographical journey and the "I-wish-I-were-white-but-never-could-be" problem. The summer after I graduated from high school in 1959, a group from our Korean Presbyterian Church once again attended a youth conference at Forest Home. Included in our group were two close white friends of mine, Rick Fries and Leroy Knouse, who had graduated from Manual Arts and were themselves very Afro-Americanized. As a matter of fact, as a testimony to just how much the color of skin didn't matter to the black majority at Manual, Rick had been Captain of the Varsity Football Team and Student Body President. Be that as it may, the three of us got to know a white guy from the suburbs that week whose first name was Steve and whose last name I won't mention. We had played a lot of football and basketball together and developed good feelings toward him.

Rick, Leroy, and I had been accepted to UCLA and began our freshman year in the same carpool, commuting daily to Westwood from South Central L.A. We hung out together at school and one day we were sitting down on the hill behind the men's gym eating lunch. All of a sudden Steve Anonymous walked by and we had a joyous reunion. We didn't know that he was a student at UCLA. As the conversation went on, he spontaneously invited Rick and Leroy to apply for membership in his fraternity. Realizing I was sitting there too, with an embarrassed look on his face, he turned to me and said, "I'm sorry, Warren, but our fraternity is for white Christians only." WHITE CHRISTIANS ONLY. Those three words actually came out of his mouth.

I was devastated. However, at that moment I was too numb to say anything. After Steve excused himself, martyr that I was at the time, I encouraged my two white homeboys from the ghetto to join the fraternity because I didn't want to "hold them back." To their credit, bless their hearts, they would have none of it. But the damage to my frail and vulnerable sense of self-esteem had already been done. It was the first time in my life at the age of 17 I had been the object of racial prejudice and discrimination personally and solely directed at me as an individual. I will never forget the cringy feeling it gave me that day. Unfortunately, it wasn't the last time I was to experience this mixture of helplessness, self-pity, disillusionment, disgust, indignation, and rage at the hands of a Caucasian male who, as an individual human being was nice enough, but one who was oblivious to the act of white racism he was committing against me as a person of color.

Were it not for the decision to seek the ministry I had made at Forest Home, I do not believe I could have survived the four bleak and trying years at UCLA. When things got bad and I was feeling low, as I often did, the thought of attending seminary upon graduation kept me going. Pressing on toward the prize of that high calling which Princeton represented to me at the time made the present bearable. The reason it was always Princeton and not some other school is part and parcel of the "Lust is blond" syndrome. All the ministers and featured speakers at Forest Home, who were like gods to me, had gone there. The thought of going to another seminary never even crossed my mind. On an unconscious level, no doubt, getting accepted at Princeton meant getting accepted by white women. Even though there were literally thousands of Wendy WASPS at UCLA, they might as well have been a million miles away in terms of psychological distance. They were taboo, forbidden fruit, and as powerfully attracted to them as I was, I never even came close to acting out my suppressed impulses. My social life was confined to the peer group I had grown up with at the Korean Presbyterian Church. I was still a big fish in this small ethnic pond, and so with the help of basketball, cold showers, a few good friends, ceaseless church activity, and the eschatological hope of one day going to Princeton, I gutted it through four long and difficult years at UCLA.

I will never forget the first time I set foot on the campus of the seminary on what was a typical September day in that picturesque small Ivy League New Jersey town situated midway between the 100 miles separating New York City to the north and Philadelphia to the south. I had yearned and burned, sacrificed and sublimated, dreamed and doted, for 5 years since I was 16, for this moment. My fairy tale had come true and I was expecting to live happily ever after. Well, as we know about the nature of reality, there is no such thing as happily ever after. The momentum of the preceding five years caused me to go around with my feet 3 inches off the ground in my first 3 ½ months there, and with the exception of the assassination of President John Kennedy during this stretch I don't remember much else. I went home to L.A. for two weeks at the Christmas break, and upon returning to the seminary I fell into a deep depression. The 6 month period between January and June in 1964 was like nothing I had ever experienced, before or since. I became virtually catatonic within the privacy of my dormitory room at 303 Hodge Hall.

The academic part of it came easily enough, although by no means was I a top student. I consider myself a reasonably smart guy but intellectually not in the same class athletically with my prowess on the hardwood as the third greatest hoopster of all time under 5'7". Be that as it may and in utter seriousness, the first half of 1964 saw me think thoughts and feel feelings which I couldn't believe I was having but was totally unable to control. I worked on the dish crew in the dining hall during my first year, so after each meal or when class was over, I would return to 303 Hodge Hall and sit motionless at my desk for hours at a time. Beginning with questions like what am I doing here, does God exist, and does human existence have meaning, the questions eventually became, why do people eat, why does the sun shine, why am I losing my mind, why don't I buy a gun and blow my brains out. Everything became absurd. It all seemed so futile. To that point in my life, I only thought crazy people committed suicide. I no longer think this way and ever since then I have considered threats by people to take their own life seriously without labeling them or passing moral judgment of any kind. In view of how deeply depressed I had gotten, I truly and easily could have done myself in. Consequently, the fact that I didn't and I'm still walking around today with both feet firmly planted on the ground, from the tip of my toes to the top of my head, I proclaim "There but for the grace of God go I."

Let me proceed now to describe a second incident which happened to me during my first year at seminary which is similar to the "White Christians only" episode. I refer to them both as archetypal experiences because they define what racism was doing to me psychologically as an individual at the time but are also prototypical for all people of color. It took place during a cold winter weekend in the Pocono Mountains in Pennsylvania. I had been invited by a classmate from school to lead a youth retreat for the suburban church in Philadelphia where he had a field work placement. While at college I had learned how to play the guitar and honed my leadership skills serving as youth director at my home church. Folk music was big then and I knew all the Kingston Trio and Peter, Paul, and Mary songs. I could sing, dance, preach, teach, shake and bake, go to my left, float like a butterfly and sting like a bee. In the pantheon of all time great church youth leaders under 5'7", I gotta be somewhere in the top three. I loved the kids and they loved me. The color of my skin was irrelevant to them as theirs was to me. They dug the fact that I was a hip dude from out west some place close to Hollywood. It was as it should be and all was well. I was relieved to be away from the seminary campus which by then had become a place that was turning me into a catatonic crazy man. The pastor of the church, whose first name was Dwight and whose last name will go unmentioned, had driven to the campsite in the Poconos from Philadelphia early on Saturday morning. He saw me do my thing during the course of the day and appeared duly impressed. After dinner he took me aside and said he felt obligated to tell me something that hurt him more than it would hurt me but it was in my best interest. I should have seen it coming but I was a very trusting and naive 21 year old then, and in truth all ordained ministers at the time seemed like gods to me. "Warren," he said, "I like you and it is clear that you are a gifted person. It would be a shame to see so much talent go to waste. You know that the Presbyterian Church is 99 and 44/100% white so there's no place in it for you. You should withdraw from Princeton immediately, transfer to law school, and move to Hawaii."

I was devastated once again. This time too, as before, when the words "White Christians only" cut through me like a knife, I had been caught completely off guard. I was stunned and speechless. I put up a brave front — don't forget the Loretta Young Show — and managed to get a few words out thanking him for his concern and saying I would think seriously about what he had told me. I did think about it too but it would be a long time before I got in touch with the anger it had generated in me. It would also take quite a while before I developed the understanding of what was really going on underneath in this incident and how it is an example of racism at its demonic and subtle worst. I recall a vignette from *The Autobiography of Malcolm X* (New York: Grove Press, Inc., 1966), which he says on page 35 of that magnificent book, became the first major turning point of his life. He had just entered the 8th grade and was one of the very best students at 99 plus % Mason Junior High School in Mason, Michigan, about 12 miles from Lansing. His English teacher, Mr. Ostrowski, who had given going-on 14 year old Malcolm Little some of his highest marks and also the impression of liking him, asked him one day what he was thinking about for a career. Reply on page 36, "Well, sir, I've been thinking I'd like to be a lawyer." Response of the tall, reddish white man with a thick mustache, "Malcolm, one of life's first needs is for us to be realistic. Don't misunderstand me, now. We all here like you, you know that. But you've got to be realistic about being a nigger. A lawyer — that's no realistic goal for a nigger. You need to think about something you *can* be. You're good with your hands — making things. Everybody admires your carpentry shop work. Why don't you plan on carpentry?"

And so it is, I believe that the Rev. Dwight Anonymous, consciously, at any rate, had positive motives in giving me the advice he did on that cold winter's night in the Pocono Mountains in 1964. But as we know, the road to hell is paved with good intentions. The incident plunged me further into the hell of depression as I was unable to tell anyone what he had said to me. Clinically speaking, depression is hostility turned inward at the self, or put a little more simply, unexpressed anger. Sex and aggression were the two areas of my life that I was the most repressed and inhibited. Of course I didn't realize this at the time and I continued to sink further into the depths of despair. There were no people of color on the Seminary Faculty then, and only a handful of racial minority students. There was no one to confide in on campus about this issue who I felt could really understand what I was going through. I had established good relationships with several white classmates, but although I was able to speak freely with them about issues regarding sexual frustration, I kept the racial identity problem wholly and completely to myself.

In the grace and providence of God, I managed to survive the bleak winter of 1964 and proceeded to witness the glory and splendor of my first of three springs in Princeton, N. J. The doctrine of the resurrection took on fresh meaning for me as I saw the signs of new life come blossoming forth in a dazzling display of colors, the brilliance of which I had never seen before. I remained clinically depressed during the next few months but the obsession with suicide began to fade the closer it got to semester's end and the prospect of going home to L.A. in June. The summer of 1964 marked a turning point in my life psychologically and emotionally. I knew then I could not solve the depression problem by myself and sought professional help. I entered therapy with Glenn Whitlock, a Ph.D. clinical psychologist and Presbyterian clergyperson, who was employed full time by the Presbytery of Los Angeles to provide counseling and guidance to candidates preparing for the ministry. I opened up to Glenn, who happens to be white but a member of a minority group as a paraplegic, as honestly and fully as I knew how. In addition to weekly individual sessions with him, he placed me in an encounter or "T" group which met weekly in the evenings at his home in West L.A. At last I began to deal with the underlying issues of sex and aggression that were the root cause of what was troubling me. I also began to see where racial factors fit into the equation although it would take longer than one summer's worth of therapy to figure the whole thing out.

I returned to Princeton for my middler year in the fall of 1964 feeling much better about life and myself. I would never get as depressed again as I did during the first six months of that year because I had learned ways to recognize and cope with this particular symptom. Suicide was no longer an option, although homicide started to enter my mind. Instead of blowing my own brains out, why not blow up Miller Chapel or the dining hall at supper time? After all, it wasn't me who I was mad at. My aggression was really aimed at the racist society which had created feelings of self-loathing by telling me to stay "in place with my own kind and move to Hawaii." While I was never to experience the "dark night of the soul" again to the same degree or intensity, the second and third years of seminary saw me in the throes of a crisis of a different kind, this time a theological one in which I thought I had lost my faith in God and therefore could not in good conscience go into the ministry.

    I had discovered techniques in the summer's therapy with Glenn Whitlock whereby I was able to escape the severe catatonic-like bouts with depression which had plagued me earlier that year. Emotionally and psychologically I developed coping mechanisms that made me a happier and healthier person — more like my Manual Arts true self. However, intellectually, I lost my faith in God. I had been a philosophy major at UCLA and taken several courses there which challenged the claims of religion in general and Christianity in particular. Nevertheless, I was so preoccupied at the time with the eschatological hope of going to Princeton upon graduation, that what I was studying then simply went in one ear and out the other. At my desk in 303 Hodge Hall, after quickly completing the regular class assignments, I turned to the existentialist philosophers I only cursorily glanced at during college and began reading them with a vengeance. Friederich Nietzsche, Franz Kafka, Jean Paul Sartre, and especially, Albert Camus, were my favorites. Accordingly, believing "God is dead," I could not possibly continue to be a Christian, much less preach the gospel of Jesus Christ and become a minister. Also, during that period, I became obsessed with two questions which would take many years to resolve, first, the problem of evil and why people suffer, and second, the problem of Christianity as the only true religion.

    In the final analysis, therefore, given my faith crisis and state of mind, I now believe it was God and God alone who kept me from leaving Princeton. As a matter of fact, since I did not find intellectually satisfying answers to the questions I was raising, in my senior year I took the Law School Admissions Test and applied to three law schools back home, UCLA, USC, and Loyola. I received one of the lowest scores of all time on the LSAT and coupled with my very average grades from both college and seminary, early in the summer of 1966 I was sent word from each of the three universities that I had been rejected. I was more relieved than disappointed. This reaction, I believe, provides a clue to what was going on at a deeper level with my so called crisis of faith. I eventually came to the understanding that my reluctance to seek the ministry was not a theological problem so much as a psychological one which had its roots in the disease of white racism.

Chronologically speaking, I graduated from seminary in early June, 1966. I did not hear from the last of the three law schools I had applied to until late in the month after having returned home to L.A. What now? I called Glenn Whitlock immediately and entered therapy once again. I had gone to school for 19 consecutive years since the age of 4 ½ and was tired. I also always had a summer job, so for the first time since junior high school I didn't try to find one. I went weekly for individual sessions with Glenn and also in the evenings as a member of a "T" group. By then I had become much better at expressing feelings of anger. My acting ability also helped me scare the daylights out of some of the white folks in that group. As Flip Wilson used to say, "The devil made me do it."

In therapy with Glenn, I came to realize that my intellectual crisis of faith in God was more psychological in character than theological. As such, there were two dynamics operating. First, it was a case of negative attention. As surely as children will do naughty things to get their parents or siblings to take notice of them, my struggle of the soul was an indirect and unconscious way to gain recognition in the seminary community. I wanted people to feel sorry for me and admire me for being such a deep and profound thinker. The fact that I was going through this faith crisis also provided me with a certain sense of identity, which might be described as something like "ex-fundamentalist-whose-faith-has-been-destroyed-is-engaged-in-noble-quest-for-God-and-trying-to-discover-if-human-existence-has-meaning."

Second and more importantly, the crisis of faith gave me an excuse to opt out of the ministerial process. Here's how it worked and how racism fits into the picture. Thinking I could no longer believe in God and therefore should not pursue ordination provided me a perfectly understandable and legitimate reason for avoiding the pain and anguish that would have resulted from my having to compete with the white guys in my class (they were all men in those days) for jobs in the Presbyterian Church that I literally knew I didn't have a "Chinaman's chance" of getting. In other words, the underlying unconscious emotional cause of my intellectual faith crisis was fear. I was afraid to get hurt again, as had happened to me twice before specifically and directly in the "White Christians only" and "Move to Hawaii" incidents, and also as had happened generally and indirectly my whole life as a person of color trying to survive psychologically in racist white America. I knew in my heart that I was as good, if not better, than all my lighter-hued classmates in terms of competence and ability. I also knew that there was no point in interviewing for jobs in the spring of my senior year, as everyone else was doing, because there was no way any church, except "one of my own kind," was going to hire me. In those days no racial minority churches sent representatives to Princeton Seminary to interview graduating seniors to serve their congregations as pastors. There were so few of us it wouldn't have mattered if they did.

The two-pronged psychological understanding of my theological faith crisis emerged as the therapy progressed. I also want to mention here that Glenn Whitlock wasn't the only mentor I had along the way, although without question he was the primary one. Two professors at the seminary who, needless to say, happened to be of the Caucasian persuasion, were very kind and helpful to me at crucial times during the course of my three year Princeton odyssey, Drs. James Lapsley and James Loder. It was beginning to become clear to me during the 1966 summer of recovery and healing that I belonged in the ministry of Jesus Christ. Aside from the weekly individual and group therapy sessions, my major activity was going to the beach every day. I have always loved the beach, especially as fall is approaching late in the afternoon, as the sun is setting and most of the people have gone. In long walks at dusk on the sands of Hermosa Beach, I began again to hear the still small voice of that same One who called me to preach the gospel 8 years before in the mountains of Forest Home.

The fact of the matter is, I realize now God had never forsaken me even though it felt that way. At my absolute worst times at UCLA, I would hop in my car and drive to Santa Monica, less than 10 minutes from Westwood. There, overlooking the beach high on the Bluff, I would stand by the rail peering out at the shore below and the horizon beyond. I remember one time in particular. Nothing mystical or supernatural happened but I know now that it was God's personal presence I experienced that day. Absolutely no one was on the Bluff because it was as cold as it ever gets in Southern California, and the wind was howling and the sky was dark and ominous. The peace that passeth understanding descended upon me then. The Creator of the unspeakably awesome beauty of the expanse below was assuring me everything would be alright. Storm and tempest may lay at the horizon of my life but "Let not your heart be troubled, neither let it be afraid, I have overcome the world." In the words of the Psalmist, chapter 73 verse 23, "Nevertheless I am continually with thee. Thou dost hold my right hand."

When times got bad at the seminary, even though intellectually I was doubting whether or not there even was a God, there were two things I did, one during the day and one at night. Princeton is located in an absolutely beautiful natural setting. There are lovely secluded woods within easy walking distance of the campus. I found a spot in back of the Institute for Advanced Studies, where Albert Einstein used to do his thing, where I would go frequently to get away from it all and commune with nature. At night I would go to Princeton University Chapel, the largest medieval cathedral in America. There, in that magnificent Gothic sanctuary sitting alone in the dark, I would listen to the organist rehearsing music that filled my heart and stirred my soul. I know now that the never-forsaking Creator was with me in those moments of stillness and meditation. It was an exercise in "looking for God in all the right places" as opposed to the "wrong places," say, like daily morning chapel services at 10:00 o'clock which I dutifully and compulsively attended. One reason life had gotten to seem so absurd for me during that six month stretch from January to June in 1964, is that as I was earnestly searching for God in my daily vigil at Miller Chapel, my never-failing and constant preoccupation during those 20 minute worship services was trying to do everything in my physical power to keep from passing gas. You see, having been raised on Korean food all my life, one can only eat so much macaroni and cheese without having serious gastronomic difficulties.

I want to move on now to mention four people from this part of my autobiographical journey. The first two are good friends of mine to this day, Gil Gardner and David Connolly. Gil I met as a freshman at

UCLA and later we attended Princeton Seminary together. From him, especially during the height of my "I-would-have-killed-to-further-my-budding-ecclesiastical-career" stage, I learned the lessons of what it really means to be a success in human life. He was right. It doesn't have much to do with power, prestige, and money. It has everything to do with love, spending time with your children when they are young, being in touch with your feelings, and having the courage to go against the grain when even those closest to you think you are a fool. David Connolly I met in my first year at Princeton. I loved him instantly from the first moment I laid eyes on him. His smile lit up my world from that time and has been doing it ever since. He is of the Caucasian persuasion from a biological standpoint, I realize, but I don't consider him as being white because he was born in Belfast, Northern Ireland. In other words, he's ethnic, which makes him "one of us." David and I roomed together for two years in 303 Hodge Hall and we have remained the best of friends since graduation in 1966. We are closer today than we were then. As an old saying goes, "You can make new friends, but you can't make old ones."

The other two people I want to mention are both African Americans, Louise Waters and Willie Henigan. I met both of them in my first year at Princeton in the kitchen when I worked on the dish crew. Willie was a cook and Louise was a "salad person." Louise became my mother-away-from-home because it was to her I would turn when the going got tough, as it often did. To be sure, I didn't confide in her the same way I did with a therapist, but I would talk to her for hours on end about real life nitty gritty issues. She kept me sane in an environment that was causing me to feel insane. Like Annie Tolliver and Carmelita Brown in the second grade, Louise loved and protected me in both direct and subtle ways from white folks who would do me harm. I know my majority classmates on the kitchen crew couldn't relate to what went on between her and me. I suppose seeing a young Korean American man and middle aged African American woman kissin', huggin', and fussin' over each other was too much for them to handle.

I admired Willie Henigan like I do Billie Dee Williams. Man, was he cool. He was a throw-back to my Manual Arts High School days. He too, like Louise, took me under his wing, and I would go into the kitchen during off hours just to talk to him. It wasn't until my senior year, however, that we started to go out at night together. I was growing less inhibited socially with the opposite sex as time went on in Princeton. White girls were still forbidden fruit, nevertheless, and basically I considered them off-limits. Willie introduced me to a variety of bars and dance halls in Trenton, about a 20 minute drive from Princeton, where my true self came out in the company of African Americans. He taught me how to drink White Label and water, and how to do the Boston Monkey. Because of him, the beautiful black women of Trenton accepted me as one of their "own kind." I did a lot of coming of age my final year of seminary, thanks to Willie, who from that time on became Billie with a "B" to me because that's what he was called in the ghetto. He will always have a special place in my heart for befriending and caring for me as he did. I consider him no less a mentor than Glenn Whitlock because he taught me about the wonders of the real world and the joy of life — after the sun goes down. I'm not here talking about sex because I remained as virgin as the driven snow. It is all about love and what God has to do with it.

At this point I cannot restrain myself from sharing another episode from the saga of my on-going non-NBA sandlot career on the hardwood which occurred during the Princeton years. This, too, really did happen, folks. Honest. I was the starting point guard all three years on the touring seminary basketball team which was a participating member of the Inter-Seminary All-Comers League. Hmm... We played other theological schools like Union (non-denominational) and General (Episcopalian) in New York City, Drew (Methodist), New Brunswick (Reformed), and also teams from both the Princeton University Graduate School and the Junior Varsity. Well, in my senior year in our gym on the seminary campus, Faith Seminary in Philadelphia beat us by about 60 points. The reason this was so special to them is that it meant that it was a victory for righteousness over evil. Faith Seminary was founded and headed by the world famous fundamentalist preacher and teacher, Carl McIntyre, who believed us liberals from Princeton were instruments of the devil because of our radical theological views. Princeton, liberal? What a joke! What made the game even more special is that McIntyre's son, Carl Junior, I think, was the star player on their team. He must have burned us for about 35 points that night.

A rematch was scheduled later in the season on their home floor. However, instead of going to Philadelphia to the campus of Faith Seminary itself, the game was played at Shelton College in Cape May, New Jersey, a four year college also founded by Dr. McIntyre, which had a much larger student body. The gym was packed when we got there. I think they even had cheerleaders. They had come to see the heathen get killed, like feeding Christians to the lions. It just so happened that we fielded about the weakest squad we had at the time. Five of us crowded into Rick Thyne's 1965 two-door Chevy Impala and made the long drive to Cape May. Rick, my Forest Home and UCLA homeboy, at 6'4" he fulfilled the stereotype that "White men can't jump" but he could shoot the eyes off the basket and once scored 78 points in an intramural game. I was on fire in the first half and scored 20 points in a tight contest. I dislocated the pinky on my shooting hand at the beginning of the second half and didn't make another basket. No matter. Another Forest Home and UCLA homeboy, Mark Rohloff, took up where I had left off and made some incredible hoops down the stretch. Now this was one white boy who could sky. We edged them at the buzzer with me dribbling out the clock like Marques Haynes. They were stunned. They couldn't believe it. They had come to the gym, both the players and their screaming fans, expecting to see Darth Vader get creamed by Luke Skywalker. To their credit, they accepted the defeat graciously. As we were leaving the floor to take our showers, I overheard Dr. McIntyre's son say to a team mate, "Pride goeth before the Fall."

Meanwhile back at the ranch, the summer of 1966 was fast coming to an end. The therapy with Glenn had gone extremely well and I had turned a psychological and emotional corner in terms of self-understanding. I was now ready to seek a call (job or position) in a church and pursue ordination as a Presbyterian minister. This is just as well because had I not decided to do so, the draft was staring me in the face. As a result, in good conscience I was able to retain my 4-D status with the Selective Service System as a clergyperson. This was the category that Muhammad Ali tried in vain to obtain as a Muslim minister but was denied. "Ain't no Vietnamese ever called me nigger," he said, and I too knew I had no business fighting for a "White Christians only" country trying to kill people who looked like me.

Early in October, my then home Pastor at the Korean Presbyterian Church, the Rev. Peter Kwon, told me that the Westminster Presbyterian Church, located at 2230 West Jefferson Boulevard about a mile and a half due west on the same thoroughfare as our little ethnic congregation, was looking for a part-time Director of Christian Education. I called the Rev. James E. Jones, Pastor of Westminster, to inquire about the position. He told me to meet him that very evening at the church. Jim was never a man to pussy foot around. When I arrived at the church, Jim was waiting for me along with Mr. Neile L. Adams, Clerk of Session and Chairperson of the Christian Education Committee. I was hired on the spot at the salary of $300 per month, which sounded like a lot of money to me at the time. I started work on October 1, 1966 and for the next seven glorious years my earnest prayer and constant cry would be, "Thank you, Jesus."

## Chapter 3

# Save Me a Seat

Let me begin this chapter by explaining where the title comes from. Westminster Church was about the last inner city congregation in Los Angeles to abandon the weekly Sunday evening worship service. We gave it up within a few years of my beginning work there. Our sanctuary had a seating capacity of about 800. The average attendance at the service was about 10 people, if that many. We would conduct a full blown service lasting about an hour in which the organist played and Jim or I delivered a regular sermon. It was like preaching into the Grand Canyon. In any case, as is traditional in large African American churches, Westminster, with a membership of over 1000 on the rolls, had an usher board. The ushers, most of whom were older adults, wore navy blue uniforms with insignia on them and white gloves. Brother Freeman B. Gates, who was also a Ruling Elder and already well into his 80's, was a staunch member of the Senior Usher Board and never failed to attend the weekly evening service, uniform and all. I can still see him walking down the aisle with his arm wrapped around his torso so that his white-gloved right hand was resting on his lower back. How I loved and was loved by that wonderful old man, who treated me like a grandson. When I first got to the church, I asked him to call me by my first name. He said, "Okay, Rev. Lee, next time." He never did address me as Warren, as is the case with all the older members of the congregation. I was always Rev. Lee to them. Well, religiously at about 6:59 every Sunday evening, just as I was about to walk up to the chancel from a small room off the sanctuary, Brother Gates would sneak a peek at me and whisper, "Hey, Rev. Lee, save me a seat."

When I first began the job at Westminster, I was all of 24 years old. It's true that the therapy had helped me work through several important identity issues, and I wasn't carrying a lot of unhealthy psychological baggage into my first church position. Nevertheless, I was still "wet behind the ears" when it came to life experience. What did I know? Compared to people like Brother Freeman B. Gates, not a whole lot. I was full of book learning, and even though I was ready to perform the duties of professional ministry theoretically, in practical terms I definitely was not anything to write home about. Moreover, as explained earlier, I had gone through a serious faith crisis the preceding 2 ½ years. As a result, I really didn't know what I believed theologically. To be sure, I could say all the right things doctrinally and in fact passed the ordination examinations with flying colors. However, I was empty spiritually inside, and while I was no longer obsessed with the abstract question of whether or not God existed, it had been some time since God was an object of worship for me and some One I talked to in prayer. In other words, I had lost my faith, and although the intellectual and emotional struggle over it had come to an end, there simply was no "it" there to pass on to others. I had nothing to give and everything to receive. In the grace and providence of God, this is exactly what happened,

The faith of the people gave me faith, especially the old folks like Freeman B. Gates. Many of them were grandchildren of slaves, and in the course of their lives had experienced unspeakable pain and untold suffering that I only read about in books. Compared to them, truly I had been born with a silver spoon in my mouth. However, instead of being embittered and cynical, as I had the tendency to be at that time with my know-it-all Princeton self, they were humble and grateful. God was a living reality to them in Whom they placed the full measure of their hope and trust. In the face of faith like this, my doubts about God's existence evaporated into thin air. It didn't happen overnight but it didn't take long. Within several months and on January 1, 1967 with my job becoming a full-time position, plans were made for my ordination into the Gospel Ministry by the Presbytery of Los Angeles and installation as Assistant Pastor of the Westminster Presbyterian Church on April 2, 1967.

I knew my faith crisis was over when shortly before Thanksgiving, Jim and I made a pastoral visit to one of the sick and shut-ins in the congregation. I will never, ever forget that first time I met Mother

Flora A. Wright. No sooner had we walked through the door and introductions made, when this 90 year old blessed saint and giant of a human being proceeded to recite the entire 53rd chapter of Isaiah — from memory. Is there any wonder why I learned to say "Thank you, Jesus" with all my heart, soul, mind, and strength? I visited her many times before she passed on to glory. It was always the same. I came thinking I would cheer her up. I came away being the one who had been inspired and uplifted. No longer was prayer an academic exercise like sending radio signals into the sky hoping to make contact with some intelligent being out there. When I prayed in the homes of Mother Wright and later Brother Gates after he got sick, I was talking to some One I *knew* was listening. Therefore, emotionally and spiritually, the turmoil was gone and I had been healed. I was now able to preach the gospel with power and conviction, and when I took to the pulpit the people of Westminster began to say, "Thank you, Jesus."

April 2, 1967 was one of the great nights of my life. I remember every detail of the ordination and installation service. Jim preached the sermon, Glenn Whitlock gave me a charge, the late Dr. Shungnak Luke Kim, who had baptized me as an infant, prayed and read scripture, my brother-in-law sang "How Great Thou Art," the anthem by the choir was "My God Is a Rock Within a Weary Land" featuring Ruling Elder Henry A. McPherson, M.D., as soloist, and last but not least, my mother presented me with the one and only gown I have ever owned and wear to this day. It had been purchased by the Westminster Women's Association as a gift to me on this occasion, and needless to say, I cherish it beyond words. 27 years later I wear this very same gown every time I preach, perform a wedding or officiate at a funeral, and walk down the aisle in an academic processional. It's a little frayed now but it is in remarkably good shape considering its age and the use I've gotten out of it. I will *never* part with it, as long as I have life and breath. The church was packed to the rafters that night with at least a third of those in attendance being from the Korean community. They had come because most of them had known me since I was a baby. They were there out of genuine love for me and also out of ethnic pride for one of their own who had made good. I was only the second person in the history of the Korean Presbyterian Church of Los Angeles, founded in 1906, to become a minister. There was also a large contingent of white folks from the Los Angeles Presbytery on hand, but they had come more out of curiosity and for the opportunity to see history made.

An article had appeared in the religious section of the L.A. Times the preceding day reporting that my ordination and installation at Westminster would mark the first time a racially mixed team ministry would come into being in the Presbytery. What an irony! In the entire history of the Presbyterian denomination in Southern California, because at that time the Los Angeles Presbytery consisted of over 250 churches including San Diego and excluded only the sparsely populated counties of Riverside and Santa Barbara, no congregation had ever had two ordained and installed ministers of a different race on its staff. This was *1967* not *1867*. The irony is, the first church to integrate was not white but black, and the combination was not ebony and ivory, as was long overdue and the way it should have been, but African American and Korean American. Westminster Church, for me, was like going back to Manual Arts High School where I was judged not by the "color of my skin but the content of my character." What I could do as a human being is what mattered, not what by accident of birth my ethnic ancestry happened to be. So it is in the providence of God, once again it was black people who loved me and accepted me for what I was. It was black people who gave me a chance to show my stuff and do my thing. White people had given me the message at UCLA that their world was for "White Christians only," and at Princeton their message was "Move to Hawaii." Black people, in the persons of Jim Jones and Neile Adams, hired me on the spot with no questions asked. The message of the African American community as a whole, ever since the second grade, has always been, "We love you, we want you, we will protect you, we will create an environment in which you can go as far and as high as your abilities will take you." Funny, isn't it?, that through the years when people find out that I served at a black church for seven years, it is the white folks who always ask about how I was treated in view of the fact that I am not an African American. It's not really funny, is it?, because black folks never ask me that question. They simply assume and know intuitively that race had nothing to do with it. This would have been true if I were of the Caucasian persuasion. Racism is not a problem that black people have. It is a white disease and only white people suffer from it.

Meanwhile back at the ranch, it's time to get back to the hardwood and share yet another episode in the on-going saga of the third greatest little man of all time. The first thing I did programmatically when I got to Westminster is organize two basketball teams, one for junior high school kids and another for adults. This act alone made me a hero in the neighborhood and a genius to the young men in the congregation. I solicited some donations from several members of the church who owned small businesses to purchase uniforms, which they were more than happy to do. Now, I was not only a hero and a genius, I became a king. That's because the uniforms were beautiful — red with white trim and WESTMINSTER emblazoned on the front. Man, only the Lakers wore stuff like that! If there were more money to be had, I could have got warm-ups. If that would have happened, I would have become a god.

When I walked into the Senior High Youth Fellowship meeting for the first time on that first Sunday evening in October at 5:30 p.m., Michael Livingston was speaking in front of the group. He was the Moderator, the Presbyterian term for all elected leaders of duly constituted groups in the church, and was doing an excellent job. Like Irish David Connolly, I loved Michael the first moment I laid eyes on him. Like David, 27 years later I love him 27 years' worth of life experience more. Since I was a bachelor at the time, naturally I was interested in all the fine looking women of Westminster, but I was too shy and lame to do anything about it. I talked a lot of trash, though, in the company of the guys, especially in the locker room about how I was going to strike on one of the foxes in the congregation. Michael was a high school senior at the time, and I encouraged him to strike as well. I suppose nowadays I couldn't do this type of thing because it would be considered sexual harassment. Be that as it may, neither of us ever ended up doing anything concrete about this situation, even so much as asking one of the foxes out on a date. We were both full of hot air. From that point on, the nickname we gave to each other, which has stuck to this day is, "Breeze."

I mention the Breeze in the context of basketball because he learned everything about the game he needed to know to become the star he eventually became, from me. It must be remembered that Michael was a student at Dorsey High School. He had also attended Audubon Junior High School. These two westside schools were considered "siddity" compared to "down home" Foshay and Manual where I had gone. In any case, the left-handed Breeze was a defensive specialist when I first met him. He ran around the court like a chicken with its head cut off and averaged about three points a contest. He worked hard, too hard, but he didn't enjoy himself. I am reminded of the first question in the *Shorter Catechism of the Westminster Confession of Faith*. Question: What is the chief end of man (sic.)? Answer: To glorify God and to enjoy Him (sic.) forever. In other words, the ultimate purpose of life is not to toil, to struggle, and to suffer; it is to celebrate, to rejoice, and to enjoy. Accordingly, God did not create basketball to play defense, She gave us this greatest of games to take the ball to the hoop. To that point in his career on the hardwood, basketball had been a labor of labor for the Breeze. A.W., after Warren, henceforth and evermore, basketball became a labor of love. His scoring average went up to about 18 points a game. Unfortunately, however, with his new found enthusiasm and confidence on the court, I could no longer beat him one-on-one. Maybe I shouldn't have told him to start shooting until his arm fell off. Maybe I should have kept my mouth shut so that I'd still have some basis in reality to maintain bragging rights over him. Hmm... Be that as it may, this leads me to recall another one of the great moments in my life, the final night of that championship season of 1971. With me on the bench as player-coach, Michael poured in 27 points and calmly sank two crucial free throws down the stretch like Kareem Abdul-Jabbar in game six of the 1988 NBA Finals against the Detroit Pistons. We did it! Our impossible dream had come true. We reached the pinnacle. It would never get better than this. When the buzzer sounded, we, the mighty Fighting Irish of Westminster Presbyterian Church, founded in 1904, for the first and only time in history, had won the World Championship of the Church Athletic Association of Los Angeles. Thank you, Jesus, and Amen.

If my ministry of 27 years as a Presbyterian clergyperson amounts to nothing else, I will always consider myself a success for at least one supercalifragilisticexpialodosius reason. I was the primary influence during Michael Livingston's impressionable, identity-forming adolescent years in his choosing to become a preacher of the gospel and minister in the church. After the manner of the one who taught him the game of basketball, like the game of life, is not finally something to endure but to enjoy, he attended both UCLA and Princeton Seminary before returning home to South Central L.A. to become ordained as a Presbyterian clergyperson. Lest I take too much credit for what the Breeze would have done with his life in the long run with or without me, I am grateful to God for being the human instrument at the time through which the divine master plan for him was fulfilled. In other words, it wasn't me, I was merely someone that was blessed to be used by the Creator in Michael's own biographical journey and pilgrimage of faith. This extends to his wife as well. The Breeze early on surpassed his hardwood mentor when it came to fox hunting. Michael is not only one of the nicest and most able people God ever placed on this earth, members of the opposite sex find him very attractive. Once he got to college, it seemed like every fine woman in Westwood wanted to join Westminster Church. He was a great tool for evangelism. To make a long story short, he met Nancy Rucker at UCLA, the best and brightest human being ever to graduate from L.A. High School. It didn't hurt that she was a 10 in the fox department either. Two more great nights in Warren Lee's life: 1) Being chosen by Nancy to escort her down the aisle the night her last name became Livingston on July 27, 1974 at Westminster, and 2) Exactly one year to the day later, same time same station, preaching the sermon at Michael's ordination service. In 1993 the Lee's of Hercules, California and the Livingston's of Princeton, N.J., where Michael is Chaplain of the Seminary and Nancy teaches elementary school, are checking in regularly with each other via telephone and the United Airlines frequent flyer program. You can make new friends, but you can't make old ones. Thank you, Jesus, and Amen.

    Meanwhile back at the ranch, the time has come to talk about the one and onliest, my father in the church, brother pastor who taught me everything I know, my mentor and friend, the Rev. Dr. James Edward Jones. Jim had class and style. Two qualities, ask my wife, which have always eluded me. Don't get me wrong. I'm a very nice and loving person, but when it comes to being cool, my children refer to me as Nebuchadnezzar Nerd. However, they better not call me Ebenezer Scrooge because just like my Dad, when they ask me for a penny, I give them a nickel, a nickel a dime, a dime a quarter, a quarter a dollar. As a matter of fact, periodically they say, "It's tithing time, Dad. Please give me 10% of whatever's on you, but make it a silent offering — no change." The Bible teaches that God loveth a cheerful giver. Well, it's true, I'm a very happy person, and I give not till it hurts but till it feels good.

I could write an entire book about what Jim Jones means to me and how much I learned from him. Suffice it to say that I believe with all my heart that God had everything to do with my seven glorious years at Westminster Church and it was part of the Plan for him to be my boss, my role model, my pastor, my colleague, and perhaps most of all, my father in the faith and steward in the mysteries of God. First things first, though. Man, could he dress! For example, in the summer, we would forego our Geneva black gowns during worship services and wear suits with clerical collars. Jim is about six feet tall and women swoon in his presence. He looks without plastic surgery the way Michael Jackson wishes he did. I'm not saying Jim was embarrassed having me stand next to him in the pulpit each week, especially when whatever I had on any given Sunday morning was covered by my Women's Association-given gown. But summer time was a different story. As his ordination gift to me, Jim took me to a tailor where he had his suits made. However, I simply could not bring myself to get one of those all-white panama suits he wore. I chose a light blue pin-stripped seersucker three-piece thing that, you guessed it, I still have in my closet today. For starters, then, Jim taught me how to dress, but I could never approach him in terms of sartorial splendor and double-breasted elegance.

Jim had presence. He would fill up every room he entered without saying a word. The single greatest lesson I learned from him was how to be a pastor. When anyone in the church got sick, he was the first one to know and the first one there. He was at his magnificent best in times of bereavement. Normally his pastoral visits would last no more than 10 minutes, but in those 600 seconds he could bring calm out of chaos, like Jesus on the Sea of Galilee. Some of the greatest memories of my seven years at Westminster were accompanying Jim to hospital rooms throughout the city of Los Angeles to visit our parishioners who lay sick and dying. His eyes would glisten as he prayed to God for healing and comfort. I was moved to the core of my being as I observed this spiritual master and pastoral genius in action.

When I first arrived at the church in October, 1966, Jim was a member of the Los Angeles Unified School District Board of Education. At that time, he had the largest voter constituency of any African American elected official in the United States. He would take me along with him to many political and ecclesiastical meetings as a kind of administrative aid. The two I enjoyed the most were first, the meetings of the then relatively small group of elected black officials in the greater Los Angeles metropolitan area. Here I met such people as Tom Bradley before he became Mayor, Congressman Augustus Hawkins, State Assemblywoman Yvonne Braithwaite Burke, who, when I saw her my knees would go weak because she was so fine and so nice, Councilman Gilbert Lindsay, and then Councilman and later Judge Billy Mills. Second, there were the meetings of pastors of large black churches in Los Angeles. These were great! Here I met unforgettable and larger-than-life legends in their own time who are still holding forth today. Not long ago when *Ebony* magazine published a survey of the ten top black preachers in America, I had met over half of them personally in these very meetings in the late 60's and early 70's. There was Dr. Thomas Kilgore, Dr. Elliot Mason, Bishop H.H. Brookins, Bishop John Adams, and Dr. L.L. White. I also met Jesse Jackson and Andrew Young during this period, although to my everlasting regret I missed Dr. King every time he came into town. Vice President Hubert Humphrey used to send Jim personal Christmas cards. He was the first person of African American descent to become President of the Los Angeles Board of Education. He lost his seat on the Board in the same vicious racist, white backlash election in the spring of 1969 when then incumbent Mayor Sam Yorty defeated Tom Bradley the first time around. The blow was softened somewhat because the weekend immediately following that disgusting display by Yorty, and the more alarming fact that it succeeded with the electorate, is that Jim flew back to Lincoln, Pennsylvania to receive an honorary Doctor of Divinity degree at his alma mater, Lincoln University. Two others were awarded honorary doctoral degrees in that commencement: the aforementioned

Rev. Jesse Jackson and the late Chief Justice of the Supreme Court of the United States of America, the Honorable Earl Warren. Lest we forget, Lincoln University, which numbers among its alumni some of the leading figures in the African American community, had been founded in the preceding century as a school to train black candidates for the Presbyterian ministry because Princeton was then for "White Christians only."

Jim knew me better than I knew myself. I had been ordained, of course, on April 2, 1967 and preached periodically since I had first arrived at the church in October. He decided to take his regular month's vacation in July and I was scheduled to be in the pulpit the four Sundays he was to be away. By then, I had developed a little common sense along with some genuine humility in the face of such saints as Brother Freeman B. Gates and Mother Flora A. Wright. Consequently, I had no intention of offending any members of the congregation and asked Jim if it would be alright with him if I preached a sermon sharing my convictions about the War in Vietnam. He looked at me and replied, "Brother Pastor, you can preach on anything you want. I'm going fishing. See you in a month."

My opening illustration in that sermon, taken from a book published by the American Friends Service Committee, *Peace in Southeast Asia*, was as follows. An American soldier is passing out candy in a public square in Saigon and children are flocked around him. A Buddhist monk passes by and forces the children to return the candy to the soldier. The soldier is puzzled and perplexed. The monk then turns to the well meaning U.S. G.I. and says, "You Americans simply don't understand, do you? You are making beggars of our children, prostitutes of our women, and Communists of our men." You could have heard a pin drop in the sanctuary where there were no seats to be saved on that Sunday morning in July, 1967. Ruling Elder Robert, R. Thompson, may he rest in peace, was the liturgist serving in the pulpit that day. At the conclusion of the sermon, he jumped to his feet and proclaimed to the congregation that my message was the most eloquent, powerful, prophetic, and passionate thing he had ever heard in his life. He asked the people to shout Amen. I didn't hear any "Thank you, Jesuses," but there were plenty of "Amens."

The very next evening on Monday, I moderated my first session meeting at Westminster (the session is the elected governing board composed of Ruling Elders of any local Presbyterian church). Was I in for a shock. After the convening prayer, none other than Robert R. Thompson raises his hand and says something is troubling him. He then proceeds to lambaste me, saying he had been deluged with phone calls from concerned members of the church complaining about the sermon I had preached 36 hours earlier. At that point, Ruling Elder Attorney William R. Freeman, may he also rest in peace, leaps in to say since the cat was out of the bag, he felt duty-bound to get something off his chest as well. Prefacing his comments with a statement to the effect that he realized I was an inexperienced and idealistic young man fresh out of seminary, and that he did not want to squelch me, he then went on in no uncertain terms to tell me that the pulpit was a place to talk about the Bible and spiritual matters, not a platform to discuss one's political views. No sooner had he spoken when Ruling Elder Gladys Wilson, who within a few months would grow leery of me because of my "liberal" theological views (although she never stopped loving me just the same), interjected, "You can't criticize God's servant!" The verbal battle raged for three hours. All hell had broken loose and I felt like crawling into a hole. Things had quieted down somewhat by the time Jim returned from vacation. At the very next meeting of the session, which was always the last Monday before the first Sunday of the following month, Rev. Jones put things in place in a hurry. He told the Elders calmly but firmly that the *Book of Order* of the Presbyterian Church unequivocally states that "God alone is Lord of the conscience." The Constitution of the denomination stipulates explicitly that no one has the right to tell a Presbyterian minister what to preach about. If members of the session didn't like it, they could go find another church somewhere which allowed them to tell their preacher what to say. Case closed. I felt like a giant that night.

My sister Aikyung died at the age of 46 in an automobile accident late on Saturday night the first weekend in December of 1968. We had a very special relationship and I loved her more than words can say. She had come to America shortly before the Korean War started in 1950. With her six year old daughter Linda, the two of them moved into our home at 3022 ½ South Vermont Avenue. Aikyung's first husband had died in Pyong Yang, (North) Korea. She remarried not long after arriving in this country, and now I realize she did this because she saw how hard things were for our family at that time. We weren't destitute and I never felt poor, but life was definitely a test of economic survival for my parents. She married a well-to-do Korean dentist, about the same age as my parents, from a little town on the Sacramento River named Walnut Grove between Stockton and Sacramento. Come to think of it, one of my fondest childhood memories is crowding into my father's 1949 Lincoln — he always loved those huge gas-guzzling cars — at 4:30 on a Saturday morning with my parents and three other sisters, and making the long, long drive to Walnut Grove on old Highway 99. We would turn right around the next day at about noon and return home about midnight. I can still see those Burma Shave signs on the side of the road.

I received a telephone call at perhaps 3:00 on Sunday morning, after I had fallen asleep, telling me that Aikyung had been killed in an automobile accident on Redondo Beach Boulevard in Gardena. Pastors hate to receive middle-of-the-night phone calls because usually it's news that someone has died suddenly and unexpectedly. I dressed quickly in my small $65 a month apartment at 2932 Hauser Boulevard, and drove to my sister's home in Gardena. She and her family had moved there after her second dentist husband had died of a stroke some eight years earlier. I waited until 7:00 or so and called Jim. He told me to come to church later that morning because there wasn't anything more I could do to help my family. The saying "Misery loves company" is attributed to Confucius, not Jesus of Nazareth. Communion was conducted on the first Sunday of the month at Westminster and this was Communion Sunday. Knowingly and wisely, Jim did not make a public announcement during the worship service that my sister had died. That would have overwhelmed me and I simply wasn't emotionally and spiritually ready to deal with a whole lot of folks. I got through the service okay but as the concluding hymn, "Jesus, Keep Me Near the Cross," was being sung, I began to crack. As inconspicuously as possible during the final stanza, I slipped out of the chancel before the benediction was pronounced. As I hurriedly walked through a corridor,

I began to cry but made it to my office with no one seeing me. When I opened the door, all the Elders of the church were standing in a circle waiting for me. Jim had alerted the session of my sister's death. When I saw them, I could no longer hold back the tears and they came rolling out as an everflowing stream. In turn, each of the 15 angels of mercy called together in that sacred moment prayed for God to be with me and my family in this tragedy. In the providence of that One who had brought me safe thus far and was not about to let me go now, two guesses who the Elders were to my immediate right and immediate left, with their everlasting arms wrapped tightly around me to keep me from falling as I wept uncontrollably: Brother Robert R. Thompson and Sister Gladys Wilson.

When St. Paul says that the church of Jesus Christ is the community of those who weep with those who weep, this is the type of scene he must have had in mind. When he says it is the fellowship of those who rejoice with those who rejoice, the scene he envisioned has got to be that great gettin' up morning, when the trumpet shall sound and in the twinkling of an eye the dead shall be raised incorruptible. I can see it now. As I approach the pearly gates, in the distance I will see my sister with Brother Robert R. Thompson at her side, waiting for me. As St. Peter checks me in, Aikyung will say, "I've missed you, little brother, you who loved me so much and was so good to me. We will never have to say goodbye again." Mr. Thompson will say, "Rev. Lee, or perhaps I should called you Warren now because equality really does exist up here, I just want to tell you that the devil made me do what I did to you at the first session meeting you moderated when Rev. Jones, I mean, Jim, went on vacation in July way back in Nineteen-hundred and sixty-seven. But by the same token, it was the Creator Herself who put me next to you that time we Elders prayed in your office after your big sister hit the center divider on Redondo Beach Boulevard in that over-sized Pontiac she was driving. By the way, Rev. Lee, I mean, Warren, she really is something special, and I know now why you couldn't stop crying and I had to hold on to you so tightly. Yo, Sister Aikyung over there, now please continue with that Korean rendition of "Precious Lord, take my hand, lead me on let me stand." Your little brother here *tried* to sing like one of us, but you can *really* do it. It reminds me of a question Brother Redd Foxx, who barely made it pass

St. Peter, once asked his T.V. son Lamont on *Sanford and Son,* "Do you know what soul is?" "Tell me, Pop, what is it?" Redd's reply, "A city in Korea." Enough of that, Rev. Lee..., I mean, Warren. It's time for you to meet Jesus. He just loves the way you shout "Thank you" and then call His name."

Another Ruling Elder at Westminster Church who took me under his wing and was as influential as any person in my life is John Grayson. There are many stories I could tell about him and what I learned from him, but let me share just one. John is a brilliant man. He is so smart and savvy, he chooses to be a member of the Republican Party. Like the character Kizzy played by Leslie Uggams in the mega hit television mini-series, *Roots,* the slave master played by the Rifleman, Chuck Connors, may have had her body but he never had her mind. So, too, the Republican Party may have John's flesh but the G.O.P. definitely never did, and does not now, have his soul. During the time I was at Westminster, he was appointed by President Nixon to serve as a high ranking officer in the Small Business Administration. He did this for a few years in Washington, D.C. and returned home to resume his post as President of Univox, an electronics firm he founded in South Central L.A. in the late 60's. An engineer by training and vocation, early in his career he worked for one of the largest and well known engineering companies in the country, TRW. He was the highest ranking African American executive officer in the company but realized in due course that there was an implicit racial ceiling to how far he could ascend up the corporate ladder. Had he stayed at TRW permanently, he would have been confined to the upper level of middle management until retirement. In any case, he traveled frequently in those days and always stayed at the Waldorf Astoria when he went to New York, the city of his birth. On one of his trips while being a guest at that world famous hotel, after having eaten dinner he entered an elevator to return to his room. He was dressed in his absolute best navy blue pin-stripped three-piece suit feeling quite impressed with himself. A very affluent looking middle aged white couple rushed into the elevator as the door was about to close. They turned to John and said, "35th floor, please."

As people of color, especially black, no matter how big we get and think we are, we will never be anything more than elevator operators to racist white America. John did not even get upset at the couple, who apologized profusely after realizing their faux pas. It wasn't their fault as individuals they said what they did. I'm sure some of their best friends are black, just like some of John's and my best friends are white. That's not the point. I'm not here referring to racial prejudice per se, the issue is institutional racism. America is worse off in this regard in 1993 than it was in 1963 or 73 or 83. Without accepting this fact and acting upon it accordingly, it is not possible to understand why Los Angeles exploded in the spring of 1992. These kinds of catastrophic events will continue to occur and are inevitable until white people as a whole — the vast majority who are not bigoted and do not harbor animosity in their hearts against colored folk — come to this realization. Racism is an institutionally-based social disease that only white people can catch. As the National Advisory Commission on Civil Disorders, 25 years ago in 1968, known popularly as the Kerner Report, put it very well, "White institutions created it, white institutions maintain it, and white society condones it."

I mentioned the name of Neile Adams in passing earlier. The time has come to say more about this wonderful Christian man and his dear wife of 54 years, Consuelo. Both Neile and Connie are pillars of the church in the best sense of the term. For years Neile has served as Clerk of Session and been a Ruling Elder. Connie has been the Church Secretary for 43 years. They are like a father and mother to me. I knew I had come home, when along with Jim Jones, Neile was the one who interviewed me for the job in the beginning. The Adams' live a few blocks from Foshay Junior High School. My older sister Sally was in the same grade at Foshay and Manual as Neile and Connie's oldest son Gregory, and my younger sister June was in the same class with their middle son Timothy. Gregory had been an All-City football player at Manual and we had sung together in the second bass section of the boy's glee club (Aeolian Club) there. In other words, in discovering all these connections, from the start we were like family. The first infant I ever baptized was their first grandchild who is now herself 25 years old, Sheila Marie, and I performed their aforementioned second son Timothy's wedding to his lovely Chinese-American wife, Kathy. Eight years ago Neile and Connie flew up to San Francisco to be "Godparents" for our son Jonathan's baptism, and four years ago I flew down to

L.A. to sit as a son in the Adams family pew at Westminster to witness my second Mom and Dad reaffirm their vows on the occasion of their 50th wedding anniversary.

Let me share just one story about my beloved Consuelo and one about my adored Neile. 13 years ago Connie was diagnosed as having terminal cancer. Gregory called me with this alarming news and I immediately caught the next plane to Los Angeles. I visited her at Kaiser Hospital on Sunset Boulevard, and she was the same "Mrs. A," which is what I called her sometimes, as always. Smiling, ebullient, and radiant, she told me how glad she was to see me and not to worry. She was prepared for any eventuality because "We may not know *what* the future holds, but we know *who* holds the future, even Jesus Christ our Lord." Like Mother Flora A. Wright years before, I went to see Connie thinking I would cheer her up. I came away being the one who had been blessed and inspired. She would stay in the hospital a few more days to receive chemotherapy. Several weeks down the road, she returned for a scheduled treatment. Much to the amazement and total disbelief of the doctors, the malignant tumor had begun to shrink, which was considered a medical impossibility. That's the point, isn't it? With human beings, what had happened was not possible. With God, all things are possible. This is not to say that if people have enough faith, they will not get sick and die. This is to believe that every day and every breath of life is a gift from the Creator. Connie is living testimony to the grace and goodness of God. At 75 she is healthier, happier, more ebullient, more radiant, more beautiful, and more youthful than ever. Age is a matter of the mind. If you don't mind, it doesn't matter.

Neile is a retired mail carrier of the United States Post Office, the greatest repository of African American talent in this land of the free and home of the brave. I recall one of Martin Luther King's proposals from an earlier era when he said the chronic problem of black unemployment could be solved if the federal government would hire all black folks out of work at the time and give them a job in the Post Office. The total cost of this would have amounted to a relatively small percentage of the annual Pentagon budget. I wonder how it would compare to the annual combined federal, state, and municipal allocations to maintain penitentiaries and jails. Be that as it may, Neile retired in 1988 after 41 years in Uncle Sam's civil service. During the time I was at Westminster, Neile delivered mail at a predominantly Jewish neighborhood in a western section of the city near the Carthay Circle Theater. He had done this six days a week for 23 years when he received word that he was being transferred to Century City. This was much better for him physically because no longer would he be required to fight those *Life* magazines in his shoulder pack, but wheel around a cart on an elevator in the high rise buildings of that famous complex next to Beverly Hills. To know Neile is to love him. He is an exceptionally bright, articulate, well read, gracious, kind, gregarious, and warm human being. Well, after 23 years pounding the pavement daily in the neighborhood, he had become an institution in that community. He was a walking door-to-door chaplain. People took him into their confidence and would share their deepest interpersonal and emotional problems with him.

When it was announced that he was being transferred, naturally they were disappointed and unhappy about the decision. However, they were also pleased to know that at his age the new route he was being assigned was much better for him. In any event, because of what he meant to the community, a special neighborhood block party was organized in his honor so people could express their appreciation and wish him well. But this was no ordinary party. Of course he received wonderful gifts and the speeches made during the program were nice. What made this an occasion for time and eternity is the surprise they presented to him at the end of the official ceremony. The organizers of the event, bless their hearts, had decided to give him a scrapbook containing greetings from people in the community. But it went much farther than that. They contacted the President of the United States, the Governor of the State, the two California U.S. Senators, two members of the House of Representatives, the Mayor of the City of Los Angeles, the State Senate, the State Assembly, the City Council, and various church groups. They all sent letters or copies of resolutions the various bodies they represented had passed, citing Neile for his years of service to this grateful community and expressing the love these people felt in their hearts for him. Racist white America portrays blacks and

Jews, like it does Korean and African Americans, as being at each others' throats. I'm not saying that there aren't serious problems between these two sets of ethnic groups, but it is not a question of ontological hate as the media characterizes the tensions. Ask Neile Adams and the people of Carthay Circle how they feel about each other. Ask him or me what *we* think about the relations between blacks and Koreans in South Central L.A. "Perfect love casteth out fear," scripture says. If the Bible does not suffice and a more contemporary document is needed, check out the scrapbook at the Adams' residence on West 38th Place near Foshay Junior High School at the corner of Western Avenue and Exposition Boulevard. Tina Turner was wrong when she sang "Love is just a second-hand emotion." Love's got everything to do with it, and in 1993 we need it more than ever. Jackie DeShannon was right: "It's the only thing too little of."

Let me bring this chapter to a close as I opened it by recalling Brother Freeman B. Gates. Brother Gates died in the spring of 1968 on a Monday. The particular day of the week is indelibly etched in my mind. The reason will become eminently clear momentarily. Jim and I visited him daily at the hospital during the last week before he passed away. He never once complained, and it was always a joy and inspiration to see him. As he was growing weaker and preparing to take leave of this world, knowing that Easter Sunday was only a few days off, he told us he would wait until the Day of Resurrection had come and gone before going home to meet Jesus. He died on Monday morning. When I was a young child, like millions of other little kids, just before I would go to bed, my nightly prayer was, "Now I lay me down to sleep, I pray the Lord my soul to keep. And if I die before I wake, I pray the Lord my soul to take." For over 25 years now and counting, my nightly prayer has been, "Now I lay me down to sleep, I pray the Lord my soul to keep. And if I die before I wake, I know you're listening, Brother Gates, wherever you are, SAVE ME A SEAT."

CHAPTER 4

# Gratitude, Humility, and Hope

My stay at Westminster Presbyterian Church came to an end early in 1973. I had begun the Doctor of Ministry program offered by San Francisco Theological Seminary in the fall of 1970. This act was to change the course of my life in a decisive way. Dr. John Hadsell, Director of Advanced Pastoral Studies at SFTS and Professor of Continuing Education, flew down from San Anselmo to Fullerton in Orange County, where the class was held, once a week to teach the winter quarter "Theology of Ministry" course. I knew he liked me but I didn't realize how much until later. Unbeknownst to me, he was paving the way for me to get a job at the seminary which would eventuate in my joining the SFTS Faculty in the spring of 1973. I had gone into the ministry to be a preacher and a pastor, not a professor and an academic administrator. In accepting the position at that time, I never dreamed it would become the major work of my professional career. Life is unpredictable and the way circumstances change and situations unfold is very interesting. That's one reason people should never commit suicide. As bad as it can get, curiosity alone should keep us from killing ourselves in order to see how things turn out in the end. In any case, I will forever be indebted to John Hadsell for bringing me to San Anselmo. I have told him so many times, and we are good friends and close colleagues to this day. He is retired now but busier than ever enjoying "the second half of life for which the first half was made."

Let me explain where the title of this chapter comes from and how it fits into the picture. The underlying idea has been present from the beginning and is a thread that runs through the entire book. The founder of the Reformed Tradition and patron saint of Presbyterianism is John Calvin. In the theological and ecclesiastical world, one of the distinctive and hallmark Calvinistic doctrines, which we Presbyterians take a lot of guff and get ribbed about, is predestination. The way in which the doctrine is popularly understood is something like this. Omnipotent and omniscient God, from the foundation of the world, has predestined some members of the human race to spend, upon their death, eternity in heaven, and others to suffer eternally in hell. Sounds awful, doesn't it? I can't speak for other Christians, of course, but if this is who God is, you can have Him (sic.), because I certainly don't want Him (sic.). This is the kind of question that I struggled so mightily over when I had my crisis of faith in seminary. Because I couldn't find satisfactory answers, everything became absurd, as absurd as this doctrine is when understood this way. It must be said, to be sure, that such an inference could be logically drawn from John Calvin's understanding of the nature of God in general, but basically everybody assumed that this idea was true in his day and age. It's like the world before Copernicus. Everyone took it for granted that the sun revolved around the earth. Humankind got quite a shock when he discovered it was the other way around.

If predestination is not about who goes to heaven and who goes to hell when they die, what is it? Let me explain. First, a brief footnote about John Calvin's *Institutes of the Christian Religion* is in order. It is crucial to realize that the *Institutes* underwent several editions during Calvin's lifetime. In the earlier editions from 1536 to 1554, Calvin discussed the doctrine of predestination under the heading of the doctrine of God, but in the final edition in 1559, it was placed under the doctrine of salvation. In other words, predestination is not ontological talk about the nature of God, it is a statement about people, that is to say, it is a confession of faith concerning how we human beings who have received the gospel (the elect), understand the way God acts in our lives.

As such, predestination is not a means to predict the future, it is only a way to understand how God's grace has operated in our lives when we look back at our past. In doing this, we come to the realization that God has been loving us and leading us our entire lives even though we were not aware of it at the time. When we look retrospectively at our past, we can see that were it not for God's goodness and guiding hand, we would not be where we are today. God has been taking care of us when we could not take care of ourselves, and this conviction in turn fills us with three things: gratitude, humility, and hope. Calvin's intended use of the doctrine of predestination had exactly this purpose in mind and apart from it the doctrine does not make sense: to engender in those who are already believe, i.e., the elect, the three emotional and spiritual qualities of gratitude, humility, and hope.

It should be clear now where the title for this chapter comes from and why. I have used the term "divine master plan for my life" a number of times before and to be more precise, theologically, it is the doctrine of predestination I have been talking about. Here's how it works. When I look back at my almost 52 years of life on planet earth, I am utterly and overwhelmingly filled with three things: gratitude, humility, and hope. God has been taking care of me when I could not take care of myself. She has been with me every step of the way. To begin with, She gave me life itself. She was there in the move of our family to South Central L.A. in 1949. She brought me through Vermont Avenue Elementary School, Foshay Junior High School, and Manual Arts High School. She called me to preach the gospel of Her only begotten Son on the mountain top one mile closer to heaven at Forest Home. She was with me as I was having "lust in my heart" for the blond surfer girls at UCLA, and let me know She had not gone anywhere that blustery winter day at the Bluff overlooking Santa Monica Beach. When I needed Her most and thought She had forsaken me, Her still small voice spoke to me in the wishing spot in the woods in back of the Institute for Advanced Studies and in the silent magnificence of Princeton University Chapel at night. She used Glenn Whitlock to help me get myself back together so I did not have to go to the jungles of Vietnam. She blessed me with Brother Freeman B. Gates and Mother Flora A. Wright, whose faith gave me faith and why I learned to shout "Thank you, Jesus" with all my heart and soul. She gave me Jim Jones, Neile and Connie Adams, the Breeze and Mrs. Breeze, John Grayson, my frayed Geneva black gown and the powder blue seersucker three-piece summer suit hanging in my closet. She caused me to apply for the Doctor of Ministry program at San Francisco Theological Seminary and put John Hadsell in my life. Is there any wonder why I am filled with gratitude, humility, and hope as I look back on my autobiographical journey, and this is only 1973?

Meanwhile back at the ranch, a whole new world came into being for me after moving to San Anselmo. I never thought I would live anywhere else except in South Central L.A., and here I was "home alone" 15 miles across the Golden Gate Bridge north of "Everybody's favorite city." I have come to love the San Francisco Bay Area and now claim it as my own, by adoption. But L.A. will still always be home. My father and sister Aikyung are buried at Inglewood Cemetery across the street from the fabulous Forum where the Lakers play basketball. Our family owns one remaining plot there and of course it's reserved for my mother. However, it gives me great comfort to contemplate the prospect of my final resting place being on a hill overlooking the scene of some of my greatest earthly memories. Elgin Baylor, Jerry West, the 33 game win streak and first World Championship in 1972, Kareem Abdul-Jabbar, Magic Johnson, and 6 NBA Championship banners hanging from the rafters. Nevertheless, I have made peace with the fact that this will never be. It's Susan and me "till death us do part." With that commitment goes a burial place somewhere with her, and she absolutely can't stand L.A. Like so many people born, raised, and living in the Bay Area, she hates my home town with an ontological passion. As for me, I'm like Ruth in the Old Testament. To my beloved Susan I say, "Whither thou goest, I will go. Whither thou lodgest, I will lodge. Thy people shall be my people, and thy God my God." At times this commitment is not the easiest thing in the world to keep, notwithstanding how fine she is, what a great salary she makes, and the fact that she is the mother of my children. As alluded to earlier, my wife is a fourth generation Chinese-American. The Chinese are into money, gambling, and most of all, jade. I, as an Afro-Americanized Korean, am into the Lakers, Jesus, and most of all, garlic. Marriage is great, though. I recommend it highly — but only to a person you can really laugh with and genuinely consider to be your best friend. In my senior year at Princeton Seminary I took a course in pastoral counseling from an agnostic Jewish psychiatrist who had us read, instead of scientific textbooks on human behavior, a series of great novels. Among them were Scott Fitzgerald's *Tender Is the Night,* Jane

Austen's *Emma,* Joseph Conrad's *Heart of Darkness,* Morris West's *The Devil's Advocate,* James Agee's *A Death in the Family,* J. D. Salinger's *The Catcher in the Rye,* and Nathanael West's *Miss Lonely Hearts.* Just the thought of these breath-takingly magnificent works makes me feel somewhat embarrassed to be attempting to write a book and having the temerity to try to have it published. There really is a lot of great literature in the world. Disclaimer aside, I mention the pastoral counseling course because a statement that the visiting instructor made in passing about the institution of marriage stuck with me. "Marriage at best," he said, "is friendship plus intimacy." If only more spouses were good friends. There would be millions, perhaps billions, of happier people and healthier children on our planet.

I served on the Faculty at SFTS from spring, 1973 to fall, 1977 in my first stint in San Anselmo. Those were good years overall, and I truly enjoyed the work I was doing and found it gratifying. At this stage in my professional career, I was still a young man on his way up. Actually, ambition was the dominant reality in my life. During my time at Westminster, I was very active at both the regional and national levels of the Presbyterian Church. In retrospect, I believe this, too, was part of God's predestined divine master plan for me. Because I achieved high ecclesiastical status early on while still in my late 20's and early 30's, I was able to get this vocational success stuff "out of my system" so that it wasn't a factor later on. I had been elected on a fluke as Vice Moderator of the Synod of Southern California at the age of 27, and before turning 30 I was Chairperson of the Synod Committee on Religion and Race and President of the Greater Los Angeles Chapter of the Presbyterian Interracial Council (PIC). By virtue of these kinds of activities, I was appointed to a national committee of our denomination, the Equal Opportunity Advisory Committee to the Department of Ministerial Relations of the General Assembly. This meant that I flew back east on a regular basis, making me feel quite self-important in those days. Since Jim had taught me how to dress, although I paled by comparison to him, the darker and more conservative suits I wore made people at airports think I was a Japanese businessman.

Preoccupied with work and career, time passed quickly in San Anselmo. Something happened after several years there that led eventually to my leaving the seminary and accepting another position. The mother of the wife of the first couple whose marriage I had performed in 1967 committed suicide. She was an old family friend in the First Wave Korean American community in Los Angeles. Her mother and my mother were the best of friends. Let me call her Mary although that was not her real name. She was a very attractive and sophisticated woman. She had everything, or so it appeared, at least, on the surface — looks, intelligence, good health, good reputation, money, family, and friends. Underneath, she was desperately unhappy because he wasn't doing what she really and truly wanted to do with her life. Her death precipitated a long and deep values clarification process within me. Here I had, or so it appeared on the surface, everything. I was a young man on his way up the ecclesiastical ladder of success with an unlimited future in front of him. Today, a national committee member, tomorrow, its chairman, within a few years, Moderator of the General Assembly, next decade, Stated Clerk of the denomination, the decade following, General Secretary of the World Council of Churches. I had it mapped out.

Mary's death changed all that. I began to ask myself the question, what is really important to me? What do I really want to do with my life? Am I really happy? Is travelling to New York constantly and people thinking I'm a Japanese tycoon the answer? No. Is attending endless meetings where I'm not truly interested in what's going on the answer? No. Is kissing the behind where the sun don't shine of people I don't even like, but am only doing so that they'll help me get ahead in my career the answer? No. What, then, *is* the answer? The answer to what I really wanted to do with my life at the time was the same as it had always been: fly. What? Yes, fly, metaphorically speaking, as in the monster best selling book of that era, *Jonathan Livingston Seagull* (New York: Avon Books, 1973) by Richard Bach. Remember that great bird? He wasn't content to be like the rest of the flock. Instead of hanging around the beach all day squawking for scraps of food and chasing tugboats after garbage, he was up high in the sky, where no seagull had gone, testing the limits of ornithological aviation. He was doing what he *loved* to do, not what he *had* to do to survive. His parents, naturally, were worried and tried to get him to be like the rest of the seagulls, because they thought he'd starve to death. As a matter of fact, my mom and dad originally tried to talk me out of going into the ministry for this very same reason. Like all Korean and Asian American parents, they wanted me to become a doctor, and short of that, a dentist or a pharmacist like my sister Kay. But I told them I was born to fly, i.e., preach the gospel, and as Jim used to say, "to hatch, match, and dispatch the people of God." Again, one reason I consider myself normally neurotic and not hopelessly psychotic in mid-life is that I had the gumption to go against my parents' will at the time.

Like Jonathan Livingston Seagull, by doing what I loved to do and not letting social pressure determine what I should be vocationally, based on concern for material needs, not only have I survived, I have flourished economically beyond anything I ever dreamed. We own a house in Hercules with 4 bedrooms, 3 bathrooms, 2 car garage, and a hot tub. True, the primary reason for such affluence is that I married well, coupled with the fact that my mother, as is very common in Asian families, gave us the downpayment for our suburban mansion. In any event, I'm doing quite well in this department, thank you, and maybe can even take early retirement if Susan gets a slight raise in pay. Jonathan Livingston Seagull discovered, because he spent all his time flying and did a lot of experimenting in the air doing things seagulls aren't supposed to do, that he could dive down from the sky, enter the surface of the water at a steep angle, and then feast upon an infinite supply of fish to fulfill all his needs for food forever. He went back to the flock to share this good news. "Impossible," they all said, "It can't be true. Why can't you be like everyone else, Jonathan?" So the rest of the flock continues to hang out at the beach and chase tugboats to this day.

I came to the understanding in and through the values clarification process precipitated by Mary's suicide that my addiction to ambition was not emanating from the deepest part of my true Manual Arts self. It was not the voice of God I was hearing. It was the collective voice of the ecclesiastical flock telling me to be like everyone else in their search for success and upward mobility. The seminary community had been good to me, and I had truly come to love and enjoy both my fellow professors and the work I was doing. Nobody could ask for a better President than Arnold Come, who was never anything less than fair and kind to me, nor a better senior colleague than Howard Rice, who, as a larger-than-life individual, was, and is, an even greater human being up close and personal than his exalted public image as an ecclesiastical superstar. But I had become restless and uncomfortable with my life in San Anselmo. Making it big in the white man's world was no longer my raison d'etre. I came to two conclusions as a result of the values clarification process. First, personally speaking, it became very clear to me that family and friends are far more important to me than career. Accordingly, I declined further invitations to serve on national committees and simply finished out my existing terms. This meant I had much more time to spend with people I truly love and in whose company I wanted to be. Second, professionally speaking, it made me realize I needed to get back to some kind of racial ethnic setting. I was one of three persons of color on the SFTS Faculty then, Robert Lee and Surjit Singh being the other two, but there wasn't a sufficient critical mass of us to make any difference in the ethos of the seminary as a whole. I was tired of being a token minority. I wanted to return to a nurturing community where I didn't feel I was constantly having to fight an uphill battle against what my current faculty colleague, Old Testament Professor Bob Coote, calls the "white male gerontocracy," also known as the "old boys' club." It wasn't long after that I received a telephone call beckoning me back to the ghetto. This time, however, it wasn't black in South Central L.A., it was a Chinese one in San Francisco.

    I began my new position as Collegiate Pastor of the Presbyterian Church in Chinatown and minister to college agers and young adults at Donaldina Cameron House in the fall of 1977. It was a disaster from the beginning. I loved the people and I think most of them loved me in return, but it was simply a bad fit. I had been trained to be a preacher and pastor in a conventional parish setting, but the job called for me to be more like a recreational director and program organizer. Furthermore, I was required to move into Cameron House itself to live on the premises on the third floor of the building at 920 Sacramento Street on a steep hill between Stockton and Powell. That was equally disastrous because I hated living in a fish bowl with the other ministers on the staff. It wasn't anything personal. At age 35 and a bachelor, I had grown accustomed to having privacy and needed space to be by myself. I simply couldn't breathe in that place. Cameron House had been founded in 1873 by the Presbyterian Church to rescue young Chinese girls caught in prostitution and other forms of domestic slavery. Through the years the mission of the agency expanded to include a full range of social services. The Presbyterian Church in Chinatown had been founded earlier in 1853, making it one of the oldest Protestant congregations in California. When the white majority in our denomination, also known as "the Republican Party in prayer," tries to say Asians are Johnny-come-latelies in the Presbyterian Church (USA) and implies we don't belong, I like to point to this example. As the case may be, a highly successful youth program was begun in 1947 at Cameron House with spectacular results. Literally thousands of young people in Chinatown and throughout San Francisco have participated in this ministry through the years. Over 30 persons became Presbyterian ministers in and through the Cameron House program, and it goes without saying much good has come out of this work. CH is a great and historic institution, but I soon realized I had made a big mistake, job-wise, and began looking for another position. It didn't take long because 19 months later I was out of there.

As unpleasant as it was for me to be at Cameron House for that one year and seven months from a professional standpoint, personally speaking I know God predestined me to go there. Why? Because that's where I met Susan. Can there be any wonder that in looking back in retrospect at this experience, I am filled with gratitude, humility, and hope? When God closes a door, She opens a window. The window to marital bliss and unspeakable joy was opened by my having gone to Chinatown. I will never regret the decision to go to Cameron House, and will forever praise and thank the Creator for sending me there. Moreover, I will always feel warmly and kindly toward the people of that community. They are a wonderful bunch of folks and deeply committed to the mission of the church. It's not their fault they couldn't relate to this little Korean dude from South Central L.A. who kept shouting "Thank you, Jesus," and would get absolutely no response. I'll give them this much, though. There were 5'5" guys at CH who brought me my hat. I couldn't believe it! It was one thing that the Breeze had surpassed his mentor on the hardwood. But these tiny Chinese boys? Get serious.

I began the job of Interim Pastor of the Sycamore Congregational Church in El Cerrito (just north of Berkeley in the East Bay) on July 1, 1979. Sycamore is a Japanese American congregation and a member of the United Church of Christ denomination. It was, and is, a small church, very similar in many respects to the Korean Presbyterian Church in Los Angeles where I had grown up. The average attendance at the Sunday morning English-speaking worship service where I preached was perhaps 25-30, if that many. The Japanese-speaking service, conducted by the Nichigo (Japanese language) pastor was even smaller and consisted of mostly elderly Issei (first generation) widows. I loved those little old ladies. Let me tell you a remarkable statistical fact about them. They live longer than any single identifiable sociological group in America. Visit any Japanese-American church in this country and you will find these special children of God there. They look fragile, walk with canes, and are hunched over with osteoporosis. But they are the strongest and most durable of the human species in the land of the free and home of the brave. It is common for them to reach the age of 100 and beyond. My mother, to be sure, is not Japanese but she is 95 years old and as healthy as an ox. Susan's grandmother, who is 96, is also not Japanese — perish the thought — she is Chinese and is perhaps the single greatest individual ever produced by her race of people on planet earth. If not the greatest, certainly the cutest and the shrewdest. I love her, as I do my own great mama, more than life itself and breath itself. Grandma Effie Louie was not born in the old country. She was born in, of all places, Weaverville, California. She gave birth to nine children and keeps track of every single one of her 32 grandchildren. She is as sharp as a tack, and as wise as a serpent and innocent as a dove. Like Mother Flora A. Wright, while she may not be able to recite the 53rd chapter of Isaiah from memory, she remembers everything else. She is a living tribute to the best of the human spirit, and makes me want to live to be at least 96 if I can be like her.

Meanwhile back at the ranch, I was very happy at Sycamore Church for the two years I was there. I will always have a special place in my heart for the people of this congregation and I know the feeling is mutual. Personally speaking, the most important and momentous event of my life to date took place during this period. Susan and I were married on January 19, 1980 in the backyard of my sister Kay's house in Rolling Hills Estates, an affluent suburb of Los Angeles on the Palos Verdes peninsula. Kay and her wonderful husband Wayne were among the first Asians to buy a home in that exclusive area some years before. There are a lot of YAPPIES (Young Asian Professional People) on that hill now — much to the chagrin, I bet, of the white folks who are still in the majority there. Since the only color that ultimately matters is green, maybe they don't mind as much as I think. Hmm... Be that as it may, our wedding was another one of the great experiences of my life. Like my ordination service, I remember every detail. As a matter of fact, many of the same people who were in attendance the night I became the *Reverend* Warren Lee came to see Dr. Shungnak Luke Kim pronounce Susan and me husband and wife according to the ordinance of God and the law of the state. I was particularly grateful for the contingent on hand from Westminster Church. Jim and his lovely wife Mimi were there, as were the whole Neile and Connie Adams family, and the Breeze's parents, Earl and Hazel, representing Michael and Nancy.

I want to say a little about my best man at the wedding before resuming my saga. His name is Douglas Lee, no relation, and we first met at Foshay Junior High School. He was born in Korea and came to America with his parents and three sisters when he was 11 years old. They lived in a small town in the San Joaquin Valley 30 miles south of Fresno called Reedley before moving to South Central L.A. in the mid-50's. Doug and I rode our bikes together to and from school every day. Something we shared in common is that both his parents and mine were first generation immigrants from Korea. I can't speak for him, but I was always somewhat ashamed of this fact and secretly envied my third generation peers at the Korean Presbyterian Church whose parents had been born in this country. Oh how I wished, like them, I could be more "American" and less "Korean." Our house smelled like kimchee, but they had cookies and milk every night before going to bed like Ozzie and Harriet. I mention this here because it's an irony that of all the First Wave boys I grew up with, Doug and I are the only two who finished college and became professional people. I'm not saying this to imply we're any better or smarter than our old buddies, it's just that in retrospect I find myself being embarrassed now by the fact I was embarrassed then for harboring feelings of resentment toward my parents and envy toward those boys. Doug is now a mega successful architect in Costa Mesa, California. I am so proud of him and cherish our friendship today more than ever. I know he feels the same way because I'm one of the few people in his life he can be completely himself with. He is so successful and so powerful, as Co-Founder and Co-President of his architectural firm, Lee and Sakahara, that he can never be sure of people's motives toward him. Like anyone in his position, he is always asking himself whether or not others are being nice to him for what he can do for them, or for who he is as a person. We used to ride our bikes together to junior high school. He and I were the only two of our First Wave peer group to hike to the top of Mount San Gorgonio in the San Bernadino Mountains, when in fact we were the only two who didn't want to go in the first place. I knew him when he didn't have a dime to his name. I would love him even if he weren't the second greatest architect of all time, just below Frank Lloyd Wright but ahead of I.M. Pei. You can make new friends but you can't make old ones.

Meanwhile back at the ranch, as the two year Interim Pastorate at Sycamore was coming to an end, I was faced with the decision of what to do next job-wise. Susan and I had purchased our home in Hercules by then and I wanted to find work close by, if at all possible. A church became vacant less than a 15 minute commute away in the affluent suburban town of Pleasant Hill. The congregation was, and is, 99 and 44/100% white, and just like those surfer girls at UCLA, it was what I thought I wanted at the time. However, at least at this point in my life, my motive didn't have anything to do with race per se. I decided to seek the position there because my family could continue to live in Hercules, I would make a very good salary, and the church appeared solid and stable on the surface. It was not one of those struggling inner city congregations I was accustomed to where only a handful of people attend worship on Sunday mornings and you have to wait to deposit your paycheck because you can never be sure from week to week if there's enough money in the bank to cover it. Late in 1980 I gave my dossier to the person who handled these matters at the Presbytery of San Francisco to give to the Pleasant Hill Church. I shall call him Mr. Ostrowski in honor of Malcolm X although that wasn't his real name. All members of the "white male gerontocracy" might as well be named

Mr. Ostrowski. He promised he would submit it, because that's what the official process called for, and I was playing the relocation game according to Hoyle. He never did send it in. I really don't think it was a conscious racist act, no more than what had been done to me by Steve Anonymous at UCLA and the Rev. Dwight Ostrowski in the Pocono Mountains. In this instance, this Mr. Ostrowski already had someone in mind — the "old boys' club" always does — for the position. And so he conveniently forgot to give my dossier to the Pastor Nominating Committee of the church. As an aside and as it turned out, the middle-aged white guy they were pushing did in fact eventually get the job. Seven or eight years down the road, there was a scandal involving this man and he was forced to resign. "Vengeance is mine, sayeth the Lord, I will recompense." As my soulful wife Susan puts it, "What goes round comes round." By the time I found out that my name had not been submitted to the search committee, it was too late to do anything about it. I was outraged and confronted Mr. Ostrowski with my anger. I'm sure he had never had a meek and mild Asian talk to him the way I did before, but by this time I could tell white people where to go and what to do with their racist, low down, no good, lying, cheating, and stealing selves.

I had never been without work in my adult life. Susan was absolutely wonderful about things and told me not to worry. Certainly, the Creator of the universe, our God our help in ages past, our hope for years to come, could find me a job. Nevertheless, the specter of unemployment was very disconcerting and unsettling for me, and this experience gives me a lot of empathy for people who lose their positions in today's era of economic retrenchment and down-sizing. What it does to one's sense of self-esteem is quite profound and devastating. Of course once again, as always, God was taking care of me when I could not take care of myself. With the door to Sycamore Church closing on June 30, 1981, on July 1, 1981 She opened the window for me to return to SFTS. I was employed at the seminary part-time until the end of the year. I began work as Associate Director of Advanced Pastoral Studies, with faculty status, on January 1, 1982, a position I have occupied continuously since then. I must say a word about my boss and colleague, Dr. Walter T. Davis, Jr., at this point. I admire, respect, and love him more than words can say. He is the current Director of the APS program and Professor of the Sociology of Religion. We have been together now for 12 years. We see each other every day. Confucius was wrong. Familiarity does not breed contempt when there's a good match. When a spirit of consideration, compassion, and compromise characterize a close relationship of any kind, there's no limit to how long it can last. I could go on and on about what Walt means to me. He knows what I feel and think about him. Lest I forget, he is of the Caucasian persuasion, but he's more "one of us" than "one of them." The main reason this is true is that he spent 19 years as a missionary in Africa. He might be white on the outside but inside he's "black like me."

I often tell people that returning to the seminary in 1981 was like marrying the same person twice. At 39 I was older, wiser, happier, and more settled than during my first stint there. All the chips on my shoulder had been knocked off for good. Truly I had come to the point in my professional life where I accepted the unforgettable line of a psychologist named Wilhelm Stekel, which was quoted to Holden Caulfield in *The Catcher in the Rye* (New York: Bantam Books, 1964) by his favorite teacher as he was running away from school: "The mark of the immature man (sic.) is that he (sic.) wants to dies nobly for a cause. The mark of the mature man (sic.) is that he (sic.) wants to live humbly for one." I knew exactly what to expect at the seminary the second time around, and I was glad to get back to what I consider a "normally neurotic dysfunctional family" environment. Both the Chinatown and Sycamore experiences had some very pathological elements about them, and quite frankly, several individuals who look just like me, i.e., Asian Americans or those "of my own kind," had treated me worse than any white person ever had. Racism may be a disease only Caucasoids can catch, but evil knows no color. Relieved and content to be back at San Anselmo, the years began to pass quickly. Thoughts of having children started to preoccupy both Susan's and my mind. We went off birth control and thought we'd get pregnant immediately. It doesn't work that way, of course, and in due time we discovered that we would not be able to have our own biological or birth children. No matter. Even before we got married, we had talked about adoption. We initiated the process with the Children's Home Society late in the summer of 1984. Almost nine months to the day later, we were on our way to the San Francisco International Airport to pick up our first child, Yei Hoon Kim, who we named Jonathan Martin. He was born on January 17, 1985 in Seoul, Korea and arrived on May 9, 1985. We received the baby that God, from the foundation of the world, had predestined us to have. Then and now, Susan and I have been filled with three things for this unspeakably wonderful and pricelessly precious gift from the Creator: gratitude, humility, and hope.

I was 43 years old when Jon-Jon, who bears his middle name after Martin Luther King, Jr., came into our home. Many of my old Manual Arts friends and seminary class mates were already grandparents. For a while, I thought I wanted to become a househusband. I could have, too, when the children were infants, but now I know as they've grown older that it would have been a mistake. A primary reason I'm so grateful today that I work at the seminary and am not a parish pastor is that I have almost no night meetings and free weekends. This enables me to live out the full meaning of my vocation as a Presbyterian minister at SFTS, while at the same time being a hands-on dad. Our second child, Jae Hee Park, who we named Rebecca Megan, was born in Kwang-ju, (South) Korea, on March 9, 1987. She arrived at the San Francisco International Airport on June 26, 1987, again almost exactly nine months to the day after we initiated the adoption process for her. She, too, was predestined by God to be ours. Very different from Jonathan in terms of personality and temperament, she runs circles around me and always seems to be one step ahead of her dad. Both our children have the effect of keeping me very humble. I can't believe how an eight year old and a six year old can reduce a 51 year old to feeling like a five year old. They are the Creator's way of getting back at us for what we put our parents through and a means to prevent us from ever thinking more highly of ourselves than we ought. What goes round comes round, now and forevermore.

In 1983 Susan's father succumbed to cancer. In 1984 my father died at the age of 86. My job at the seminary made it possible for me to be a hands-on son-in-law to my wife's family and a hands-on son to my own family of origin in Los Angeles. I worked extremely hard at SFTS but it was not emotionally and spiritually draining to the same degree or intensity as life in the parish. I had come to the point where I could perform my duties on a nine to five basis blindfolded. This I did happily and gratefully, albeit without a great deal of passion and sense of excitement. The "marrying the same person twice" syndrome also played a factor here. Again, in retrospect I believe this was part and parcel of God's predestined divine master plan for my life because it allowed me to give priority to family responsibilities when my involvement was most needed. During my first stay at the seminary in the mid-70's, SFTS had established a formal partnership with the Presbyterian College and Theological Seminary in Seoul regarding the Doctor of Ministry program. Every year significant numbers of pastors from Korea came for the six week D.Min. summer term in San Anselmo. As many as 20 would be in residence, and I taught a seminar for them on formulating a dissertation topic proposal. Through the years I assisted many Korean pastors to develop their doctoral projects and was their primary spokesperson and advocate on the SFTS Faculty. Naturally they were, and are, very grateful to me although I simply was doing my job and sincerely did not think I deserved any extra credit for my efforts. In those days my Korean language ability was very limited. Although I could understand simple sentences because I had heard Korean spoken at home growing up, I could only say a few words. There was no way I could carry on a conversation even about everyday matters, and a discussion on academic concerns or theological issues was out of the question. The fact that I could not communicate in the language of my ethnic and cultural heritage did not bother me at this stage in my life, professionally or personally. My job didn't really require that I know how to understand and speak it, only that the Korean pastors have sufficient ability to tell me how I could help them in English, which they did. Even now, although my Korean is dramatically improved over what it was then, they don't need me for *it* — no matter how good I get, because I can never be as good as they are even if I studied it 24 hours a day for the rest of my life — they need me for my English. I accept this fact for what it is and consider my ability to use the English language — not that it's all that great when compared to other native English speakers — as God's gift to me, by accident of birth in this country, to share with them so they can achieve their academic goals in order enhance their ministries in Korea.

Be that as it may, the time has come to mention a man named ChangBok Chung and explain how he fits into the picture. I first met ChangBok in San Anselmo just before the fall semester was set to begin at SFTS in 1974. He had been in Decatur, Georgia at Columbia Theological Seminary completing a Master's degree in practical theology. He entered our Doctor of the Science of Theology (STD) program, which he finished in 1978. He served a Korean church north of San Jose in a community called Mountain View for several years and then returned home to Korea to become Professor of Preaching and Worship at the Presbyterian Theological Seminary (PTS) in Seoul. We became close friends during my first stint at SFTS. As a promise to my mother, he began tutoring me in the Korean language. He's several years older than me and according to Korean custom, even though I was an authority figure for him on campus, he related to me in private and interpersonally as an elder brother. After I returned to SFTS in 1981, he became the coordinator a few years later for our Doctor of Ministry program done in partnership with PTS in Seoul. Because of this responsibility, he came to San Anselmo every year for the six week summer term. From the beginning of his annual trips, he tried to get me to visit Korea so that the students I had helped through the years over there could express their appreciation to me. He also felt a sense of personal obligation because of what I had done for him during his stay at San Anselmo. I had been to Korea twice before, first in 1970 and again in 1977, taking my then 78 year old parents as an anniversary gift in honor of 60 years of marriage. Consequently, I did not have a strong desire to visit and kept finding excuses not to go. By and by, I could not put my *Hyungnim* (the term Koreans use when addressing an older brother) off any longer and finally I agreed to a whirlwind 10-day itinerary he put together for me in the spring of 1987. By then Jonathan had been with us for two years, and we had received word that Rebecca would be coming soon. For that reason, I was even less enthusiastic about making the trip because I did not like the idea of spending time away from home. Little then did I know what was in store for me in my ancestral homeland. At age 45 I thought I had pretty much resolved all my ethnic identity problems and would not have predicted, if my life depended on it, the experience I was to have on day number 8 of that incredible journey.

From the moment I stepped off the plane at Kimpo International Airport in Seoul, each place I visited and each person I met had the effect of putting the remaining pieces of the then 45 year old puzzle of my life together. The feelings that were generated in me were uncanny and awesome, unlike anything I had experienced before. This underlying "Everything was meant to be" motif is portrayed very nicely in a contemporary film starring Danny Glover entitled *Grand Canyon*. I recommend it highly, and it's available on video tape. In any case, on the long 12 hour flight going over, I was feeling resentful and unenthused about the prospect of having to spend 10 days somewhere I really didn't want to be. More often than not, this is the way the pilgrimage of faith unfolds, if you haven't already noticed. A favorite book title by a Presbyterian minister, Robert Hudnut, says it all, *Surprised by God*. ChangBok had carefully planned my itinerary and I was treated like royalty everywhere I went. I appreciated this aspect of the trip — who wouldn't? After all, the chief purpose of life is to glorify God and to *enjoy* Him (sic.) forever. Right? To be sure, this is not the same as hedonism. I don't believe human beings were put on this earth to maximize pleasure, minimize pain, and "to eat, drink, and be merry for tomorrow we die." However, there's nothing wrong with creature comforts, for my money, as long as we don't take them too seriously and make them, in the words of a great theologian from a previous era, Paul Tillich, our "ultimate concern." That aside, everywhere I went, a minister who was either a current D.Min. student or a graduate, met me and took me to his — they were all men then — church or place of ministry. In this way, I was able to see, with my own eyes, the fruits of my labor through the years. The dissertation/project topic proposals I had help shape on paper came alive in the real world. Our SFTS D.Min. folks were engaged in crucially vital and strategically important ministries. Their work was not only exciting and challenging, collectively it was serving the needs of hundreds of thousands of people and transforming the very fabric of Korean society in the name and for the sake of Jesus Christ. I was overwhelmed. I was staggered. I was thrilled. Julius Caesar once said, "I came, I saw, I conquered." Well, being treated like a Roman Emperor, I came, I saw, but instead of conquering, I cried.

Two days before I was scheduled to return to San Francisco, I visited the beautiful island off the southern tip of Korea called Cheju. The island has a long, colorful, and painful history and occupies a special place in the hearts of the Korean people. It resembles Hawaii physically and similar to the Aloha state is a favorite honeymoon spot. The Rev. Chang Geun Kim and the Rev. Young Taik Chung, two D.Min. candidates who since graduated, met me at the airport. They took me to a penthouse restaurant in the best hotel on the island, where I was to stay that night, and hosted me for lunch — *kalbi* (barbecued short ribs), *bulgoki* (barbecued beef), *namul* (seasoned vegetables), many different kinds of side dishes called *panchan*, and of course, the quintessential Korean food item, *kimchee* (fermented, garlic-laden cabbage which may be bad for your breath but good for your body and soul). The two of them then took me on a round-trip tour of that magnificent island. As we were driving up the most famous landmark and highest point on Cheju, Mount Hallasan, even though it was April, snow began to fall. The sight took my breath away and was as beautiful as anything I had ever seen. Apparently, late spring snow storms are common there, and they decided to stop at a small roadside cafe at the summit. They proudly introduced me to the proprietor, calling her *Ajumani* (something like "Auntie" which is the term used to address adult women). We had a cup of hot ginseng tea to warm up. The snow subsided as suddenly as it had started, and after getting back in the car we made our way down to Cheju City. We had dinner at a fancy Japanese restaurant, feasting on many different kinds of sashimi (raw fish). After the meal, we went to Rev. Kim's church, the Young Nak Presbyterian Church of Cheju-do ( the suffix "do" meaning island), where I gave the sermon. I wasn't fluent enough to preach in Korean yet, so my message was translated sentence by sentence as I spoke in English. I returned to the hotel after the worship service, exhausted but exhilarated.

There, in the privacy of my hotel room, as I was preparing for bed, the impact of the preceding eight days hit me like a ton of bricks. I didn't have any supernatural visions and what followed was not mystical. But as surely as the Pope is Catholic, a bird can fly, snakes have hips, and grits be greasy, it was a divine revelation. All the ripples of my life came together in an instant, in the twinkling of an eye, in that single sacred moment. I was blind, now I could see. I finally got the point. At last I knew why God had created me as She did. From the foundation of the world, before I was formed in my mother's womb, and speaking of twinkling, before I was a twinkle in my daddy's eye, the Creator had *predestined* me to be Korean. I fell to my knees and was overcome with emotion. I wept, and wept, and wept. I was filled to overflowing with three things: gratitude, humility, and hope. God Godself was telling me that this is the moment I had been created for. This is what I had been taken care of all these 45 years, through many periods and varied circumstances when I could not take care of myself, to do and to be.

I never did get to sleep that night. I cried until I had to take a shower before getting picked up early the following morning, for still another sumptuous meal. The reason I couldn't fall asleep and stop crying is that people and events kept flooding into my mind, from birth to that present moment. I saw where everybody and everything fit into the big picture. They had all been part of God's predestined divine plan for my life. Even the rotten individuals, those who had done me dirt, had been put there for a reason. If it weren't for them, I wouldn't be where I was. It was a very cleansing and purifying experience. I forgave each and every person in the past who had ever wronged me. It was a long list.

I want to single out one person in particular who warrants special attention. He is a member of the "white male gerontocracy," a Mr. Ostrowski I think his name was, the one who forgot to submit my dossier to that suburban church I thought I wanted to go to before returning to San Anselmo in 1981. I forgave him more quickly and more easily than anyone else. Just imagine if I were to have gotten that job. I'd probably still be there because I preach so good, and as a disciple of Dr. Martin Luther King, Jr. I treat everybody according to the content of their character and not the color of their skin. In other words, those white folks would have come to love me and I would have come to love them. But if that would have happened, none of the above would have come to pass. I would still be able to say only a few words in Korean and be going to monthly meetings of the Rotary Club in Pleasant Hill. And so in gratitude, humility, and hope, I have a message to give to Mr. Ostrowski should he read this book wherever he is, "Thank you for *not* saving me a seat."

    I want to say something about my mother at this point. She has been such a dominant influence in my life, and like the old gospel hymn about Jesus, my great mama is all the world to me. She was born in Pyong Yang in 1898, attended a women's seminary and became a well known women's evangelist in the Presbyterian Church of Korea in those days, even preaching the gospel in Manchuria during the Japanese colonial period, in the company of a famous revivalist, the Rev. Kim, Ik Doo. As mentioned earlier, my parents were married in 1916 and my father immigrated to America in 1922. My mother eventually came to this country herself in 1939, and after giving birth to three children in addition to the three she already had, began work at the age of 46 as a seamstress in a sewing factory in downtown Los Angeles. She is probably the first Korean woman to be ordained as a Ruling Elder in the Presbyterian Church in America.

    I acquired an overwhelming sense of gratitude from my mother. When I was a young boy, she would awaken me each morning with a vibrancy and zest for life that literally was like having a "born again" experience every day. She gave concrete meaning to the wonderful passage from Psalms 30:5: "Tears may flow in the night, but joy comes in the morning." My mother was a gifted preacher and dynamic public speaker in her day, and was well known in the First Wave Korean American community in Los Angeles. She had every right to feel frustrated and bitter about her life in America compared to what she had left behind in Korea, but she never complained and always looked to the future in gratitude and hope. My father used to say about my mother, "Syngman Rhee would have her killed if she went back to Korea, because if she returned, the people would elect her President." She really was a great orator and leader. At age 95, she is in excellent health and lives comfortably with my younger sister June in Torrance, California.

    Meanwhile back at the ranch, since the spring of 1987, the years have passed quickly. During this stretch my Korean language skill has gradually gotten better and better, and my knowledge of Korean history and culture has increased significantly. I have made 8 trips back to the homeland since the 1987 "conversion experience," and even preach in my native tongue when I go there. Ever since then, I have had great zest and zeal for my work at the seminary. As I mentioned before, I was relieved and happy to get back, but my job had become routinized and passionless. All that changed after the spring, 1987 trip. I knew, and know, God predestined me to be there. I'm exactly where I'm supposed to be vocationally, and I am filled with gratitude, humility, and hope every morning as I drive my 1979 Honda Accord with 239,773 miles on it across the Richmond/San Rafael Bridge from Hercules to San Anselmo.

This brings me to April 29, 1992. I couldn't believe my ears when I heard the news of the Rodney King verdict. Like the summer of 1965 and the Watts Riots, I was not surprised about what happened in its immediate aftermath. L.A. had exploded once again. I don't think it's difficult now for the readers of this book to understand what was going on inside me emotionally and spiritually when I saw the tragic events taking place in Koreatown. As one Korean shop after another went up in flames, and the media portrayed Koreans and blacks as if they were Israelis and Palestinians, my heart grew heavier and heavier. As I have witnessed relations between my two communities of origin and identity continue to be characterized in racist white America as they are, I have felt compelled to do something about the situation. For a long time I didn't know exactly what that something might be, but this book is one concrete result of my agony and struggle over this question. Let me turn my attention now to the problem itself.

CHAPTER 5

# Divide and Conquer

I have entitled this chapter "Divide and Conquer" because it is the way white racism works in this country against people of color. It was actually a self-conscious and deliberate strategic tactic used historically by white European nations to maintain colonial rule in the lands they were occupying. Perhaps the clearest example of this dynamic and how well it worked is the British in India. A primary reason so few were able to control so many for so long is that those shrewd White Anglo Saxon Protestants — nobody ever said they weren't smart — forced the linquistically diverse provinces of that dazzlingly wondrous but exceedingly complex land, comprised of tens of thousands of villages, to communicate in English. From half way around the world with a relatively small contingent from the home base, they were able to keep hundreds of millions of people at bay for decades. But along came a man named Gandhi, and the rest, as they say, is history. Like Abraham, Martin, and John, the great Mahatma, too, was felled by an assassin's bullet, but even though another dreamer was killed, his dream could not be destroyed.

While I do not believe that there is any kind of organized and systematic effort to "divide and conquer" racial minority groups in this country as a self-conscious and intentional colonial tactic, a primary defining characteristic of white racism is the way it affects the relationship of these several groups to each other. Mass media is the chief culprit in promoting and perpetuating this problem. I am not saying that the people who control the sources of information and channels of communication in our society are doing this with evil intent and malice of forethought. What I *am* saying, though, is that they are racist without realizing it. Accordingly, they are more dangerous to people of color than if they were outright bigots who knew exactly what they were doing. I know that the majority of people who work in the mass media from top to bottom, just like the vast majority of the tens of millions of white people in our nation as a whole, do not belong to the Ku Klux Klan. They are not Aryan supremacists who harbor prejudice in their hearts against dark-skinned folks and have never knowingly discriminated against anyone. This is not the point. It is not about personal morality, and whether or not someone is a nice person. Many years ago, the most influential American theologian of his generation, Reinhold Niebuhr, wrote a pioneering book, *Moral Man and Immoral Society* (New York: Charles Scribner's Sons, 1932), that captures this idea. Niebuhr was right then, and he's right now.

The fact of the matter is, most media folks seem to be left-of-center liberal types who see themselves as champions of racial justice. Some of these persons' best friends, I'd bet my bottom dollar, are black — the Mel Gibson-Danny Glover ebony and ivory syndrome. Consequently, they don't see themselves as part of the problem. Nonetheless, for my money, they *are* the problem. I happen to like Dan Rather, Ted Koppel, and Tom Brokaw. If I knew them personally, our relationship would be governed according to character content not skin color. I think we'd get along just fine, thank you. But people like these three are absolutely *killing* us. In believing so adamantly, as they do, that they are reporting and presenting the news "objectively," they become our worst enemies. I've seen it happen many times watching larger-than-life network news anchormen on T.V. (I use the masculine plural pronoun advisedly here because white media superstars like Barbara Walters, while sharing the same racial views and thus inflicting the same damage on us minorities as their male counterparts, are qualitatively different when it comes to feminist consciousness and as a result do not harm that disenfranchised group of human beings called women in the same way they do us). Oprah Winfrey, because she is an African American and more importantly, tuned in on this score, cannot be placed in this category (I realize technically she is not a news anchorperson). Although I like Connie Chung too, and take ethnic pride in her as an Asian American, I can't say the same thing about her.

And it's not because she's married to a white guy, either. Let me cite a typical and classic example of what I'm talking about. A few days after the Rodney King verdict and Los Angeles had exploded, Ted Koppel interviewed several key black and Korean leaders on his nightly ABC news program, *Nightline*, to discuss the relations between the two groups. A wonderfully articulate attorney, Angela Oh, who had emerged as the principal English-speaking spokesperson for Korean Americans vis-a-vis the general public, appeared on the show. She tried mightily and tactfully to get Ted to understand the role mass media plays in exacerbating the tensions between the two communities. He never got the point. They never do.

Speaking of the media coverage during the course of the riots, I want to single out the story of the Latasha Harlins tragedy. She is the 15 year old African American girl who was shot and killed by a Korean immigrant grocer, Soon Ja Du, in a hassle over a bottle of orange juice worth $1.79. This incident had taken place on March 18, 1991, over a year and five weeks prior to the day the uprising began. The problem is, the tape of the horrifying and gruesome murder was shown as though it had happened yesterday. It was aired repeatedly by local television stations and the ABC affiliate in particular. As a mater of fact, the tape was the second-most played video (next to the Rodney King beating itself) during the week of the riots, according to the media-watch section of *A Magazine* (Vol. I, No. 3: p. 4). This information is documented in a brilliant essay, "Home is Where the *Han* Is: A Korean American Perspective on the Los Angeles Upheavals," by Professor Elaine Kim of the University of California at Berkeley Department of Ethnic Studies. It appears in a journal entitled *Social Justice*, Vol. 20, Nos. 1-2 (Issues 51-52, Spring-Summer 1993), and I believe every single person in our country ought to read it.

Why did the *Los Angeles Times* and the electronic media, where, as everyone knows, in the words of Marshall McLuhan, "The medium is the message," keep harping on the Latasha Harlins incident? Because those left-of-center white liberal types, who control the sources of information and channels of communication in our society, decided to do it. That's why. I'm not saying they had conscious motives to divide and conquer blacks and Koreans, but inescapably this is the result of what they did. Why, then, you ask, would they do such a terrible thing? Because they are racist without realizing it. I cannot say make this point strongly enough and will continue to harp on *it*, until the Dan Rathers, Tom Brokaws, and Ted Koppels get the message. Obviously they haven't yet because black-Korean relations continue to be depicted and stereotyped in the same reprehensible ways.

What I mean in this instance by my giving the media moguls the benefit of the doubt in contending that they are racists without realizing it, as opposed to writing them off as just plain evil, is, *I* honestly believe that *they* honestly believe their decision to show the tape of Latasha Harlins being killed over and over again was not based on a conscious motive to inflame and damage the relationship between Korean and African Americans. To them, it was a case of "objective" reporting. It was newsworthy, given what was going in L.A. at the time. They were only doing their job. I am convinced, at least to myself, that I *do* know what in fact was going in their minds consciously and why they decided to keep airing the tape. The truth is, they want people to watch their shows. It's as simple as that. Their motivation is ratings. They will do anything, including giving away their mamas and their own soul, to win the Machiavellian war to be number one. If it means dividing blacks and Koreans so that they are conquered by an internal colonial system which keeps both themselves, as haves, and racial minority groups, as have nots, in their proper place in the social hierarchy, so be it. Sensationalism sells. Sex sells. Violence sells. They are as American as apple pie.

The reason the showing of the Latasha Harlins tape was so pernicious is that every time it played it made black people hate Koreans. The media can deny all it wants that this was not their intent, but there is no doubt in my mind that this is in fact what happened. Likewise, every time the tape was played, Koreans collectively felt guilt and a sense of personal responsibility for an act that was committed by a single individual who happened to be a member of the same ethnic group. No Korean I know has tried to justify what Soon Ja Du did. It was inexcusable, heinous, and unbearable to watch. Furthermore, speaking for myself, I was morally outraged and considered it an unconscionable affront to my African American sisters and brothers when Ms. Du's verdict of voluntary manslaughter was announced, followed by the unbelievably lenient sentence of five years probation. It is not that I wanted to see the book get thrown at her and see her suffer in prison, it's a question of justice. When such a miscarriage of it took place, I was dismayed once again by a racist society that sent a message to its black citizens that their children's lives are worth no more than a $1.79 bottle of orange juice. But it wasn't the fault of the Korean race and the Korean American community that Latasha Harlins was killed and her murderer was set free. Nevertheless, the fact of the matter is, the repeated showing of the tape had the effect of making the public feel this way. I defy the media moguls to prove otherwise. It sowed the seeds of racial hatred and pitted one racial minority group against another. If this is not what the colonial tactic of divide and conquer is all about, I don't know what is.

I would not have bothered to bring up the Latasha Harlins story if media racism had come to an end after the Los Angeles upheavals. The problem is, there has been no change in the way relations between blacks and Koreans are portrayed. It is as bad as ever. All people need a built-in "crap detector" to tell them something doesn't smell right. The aroma of feces always hits me when I see another article in the newspaper or piece on television about an African American boycott of a Korean store. Because sensationalism sells, only events of this kind, showing the two groups in their worst light at each others' throats, receive media coverage. As a person who grew up in both the Korean and black communities, I am aware of any number of grass roots programs aimed at bringing about reconciliation and healing, particularly on the part, I'm proud to say, of Protestant churches. These efforts, however, are not deemed newsworthy, get no publicity, and therefore the general public is totally unaware of them. Nevertheless, they continue to go on, quietly but steadfastly. My dream for South Central is really rooted in the people, both black and Korean, who are engaged in this mission of faith and love. In gratitude, humility, and hope I praise the Creator for these unsung heroes and heroines. The future belongs to these ambassadors of good will, not to the merchants of hate who seek to divide and conquer us in order to maintain the status quo. Martin Luther King, Jr. was fond of saying "Truth crushed to earth will rise again." He often quoted James Russell Lowell's words,

"Though the cause of evil prosper, yet 'tis truth alone is strong; Though her portion be the scaffold, and upon the throne be wrong. Yet that scaffold sways the future, and behind the dim unknown; Standeth God within the shadow, keeping watch above His (sic.) own." The Psalmist says, "Tears may fall in the night, but joy comes in the morning." "Let not your heart be troubled, neither let it be afraid, I have overcome the world." "We *shall* overcome some day."

I want to move on to examine some specific ways we Koreans are depicted in the media which are as insidious as they are hackneyed. As a result, I dare say that the images projected through the various channels of mass communication in our country are in fact how the American public as a whole, including black folks, perceive us. Accordingly, this is the reason leaders in the Korean community organize protests against the stereotypes of our people in such movies as Michael Douglas' *Falling Down* and Eddie Murphy's *Boomerang*. Again, the way the media reports these protests is part of the problem. The message that is communicated is, why are these militant activists making such a big deal out of nothing? Don't they have anything better to do with their time. After all, everyone knows that trigger-happy Korean shopkeepers tote guns and will kill over a $1.79 bottle of orange juice. Furthermore, it's common knowledge that Koreans are a bunch of strange, rude, money-grubbing, poor English-speaking ingrates who will cower before a disgruntled white man whose country we have no right to belong in the first place. Can there be any denying that this caricature is anything but the truth, the whole truth, and nothing but the truth? If the general societal understanding of our people were that we are just like any other group of normally neurotic human beings in the world — some good, some bad, we eat, sleep, get mad, go to the bathroom, etc. — protests of racial stereotyping in the media would not take place because there would be no need for them. As it stands, the image of Korean immigrants, created and perpetuated by mass media, is so distorted and pervasive, they are both necessary and inevitable.

The fact of the matter is, because relations between blacks and Koreans in urban areas had been presented in such a bad light from the early 80's on, with the attendant negative stereotyping of those sneaky and inscrutable foreigners being what it was, there was no where near the public sympathy that ought to have been generated for the Korean victims of the riots as was warranted by the magnitude of their suffering and loss. Instead, the feeling was, they "had it coming." They only got what they deserved for being the kind of people they are. Even some other Asian American individuals, who should have known better, tried to disassociate themselves from us. As Elaine Kim documents in her penetrating essay I cited earlier (page three in the *Social Justice* journal), according to one Chinese American reporter assigned to cover Asian American issues for a San Francisco daily, it was claimed that Chinese and Japanese Americans, unlike Koreans, always got along fine with African Americans in the past (Chung, 1992). "Suddenly," admitted another Chinese American, "I am scared to be Asian. More specifically, I am afraid to be mistaken for Korean" (*Los Angeles Times*, May 5, 1992). Granted these two sentiments were not representative of the other Asian American communities as a whole (Chinese, Japanese, Filipino, Vietnamese, Pacific Islanders, Thai, Laotian, et. al.). The point is, the media portrayal of Koreans and the attitude it created in people's mind toward us put all Asians on the defensive. So much for guilt by association. The bottom line is this. I am not making a mountain out of a mole hill in decrying how we are depicted and perceived as a faceless "yellow peril" in racist white American society. Our country is a dangerous enough place to live in as is. How many more Korean merchants have to be shot and killed in South Central L.A. and there is no public outcry because the underlying sentiment is they "have it coming" to them? How many more Korean shops will have to go up in flames the "fire next time" before the media gets the message?

Especially for the benefit of Korean immigrant and other Korean American readers of this book, I want to turn my attention next to several ways white racism works against black people, as I have encountered and reflected upon them in my own experience. In doing this, I hope to expose what I believe are the ultimate and final causes of the riots. If these problems aren't addressed, what happened in Watts in 1965 and again in South Central L.A. in 1992 will happen again. This is not an apocalyptic threat. It is simply a chronological prediction. The "fire next time" is only all too real a genuine possibility. Be that as it may, my contention is that the so called black-Korean problem, which is the focus of this book, is not really a problem. It will disappear as soon as Korean shopkeepers move out of African American neighborhoods, which they are doing in a hurry. The evils I will discuss presently, however, are chronic and will not go away. Derrick Bell in his incredibly powerful and compelling best seller, *Faces at the Bottom of the Well*, maintains they are permanent. He's probably right, but I hope he's wrong. Here goes.

In my view, racism, in the final and ultimate analysis, is rooted in fear. This fear, in turn, comes out of unresolved problems in white people — particularly on the part of the "white male gerontocracy" — in two areas, sex and aggression — thank you, Sigmund Freud. The myth of black sexuality is well known although it is a taboo subject. I refer one and all to chapter seven of Cornel West's *Race Matters* for an update and cogent analysis of the issue. I simply want to point out that it makes white men fearful of black men. It creates profound insecurity in Caucasian males stemming from their self-perceived inferiority when it comes to sexual virility in comparison to their allegedly more well endowed darker-hued competitors. Untold numbers of African American men have been lynched and castrated in the history of our country because of the power of this myth. As such, my first contention is that a primary reason for white fear of blacks is rooted in the sexual dimension. The second dominant cause is the aggression factor. White people are afraid that black folks, especially young men (defined as teenagers through perhaps the late 20's), are out to do them physical harm. It may sound simple but it is not simplistic. Sometimes the truth is simple, and in accepting it on face value we are set free. The Bible teaches that "Perfect love casteth out fear." After all that's said and done, this is one of the simple truths that I'm trying to get across in this book. It applies to everyone as well, not just Koreans and African Americans. I also want to add a point about white women. I don't believe the myth of black sexuality affects them in the same way as their male counterparts. It makes them sexually attracted to black men, which of course makes white men even more afraid of, and angry at, black men. However, as far as the aggression factor is concerned, I believe the psychological dynamics are the same.

With this racism-is-based-on-fear-which-is-rooted-in-sex-and-aggression paradigm in mind, I want to analyze what I believe made the jury in the Rodney King trial do what it did. Unrecognized fear makes otherwise rational and normal people crazy. Look at what my fear of getting hurt by white society did to me when I was a seminary student. First, it made me want to kill myself. Second, it made me stop believing in God. Third, it made me think I couldn't become a minister. What it made the members of the Simi Valley jury do is to distrust what they saw with their own eyes in the videotape of the police beating up Rodney King. I don't care what other kind of evidence was presented by the defense in the trial. Tens of millions of people saw repeatedly what happened to this lone black man. I would say the same thing about the Latasha Harlins tape and the Reginald Denny tape. What you see is what you get. Soon Ja Du was guilty of murder. The men who savagely beat up that innocent truck driver at the intersection of Normandie Avenue and Florence Avenue in South Central L.A. are as guilty as the cops who ravaged Rodney King. The crime is one thing, however, and the punishment another. It doesn't make me feel personally crazy that Ms. Du received as lenient a sentence as she did. Likewise, whatever happens to those who attacked Reginald Denny, I hope the book is not thrown at them (since I first wrote these words, the matter has been legally resolved, but I leave what I've written as is because the outcome of the trial didn't change the point I want to make). I am in no way, shape, or form trying to rationalize what they did. It is a matter of putting the incident in its rightful social context. I wonder how many times these young men were stopped themselves by the police at night for doing nothing — and no hidden camera was clicked on to see what happened to them. I wonder how many times they applied for a job and were told to come back later. I wonder how many times they were humiliated in front of their classmates by a teacher at school. I wonder how many times our racist society violated their humanity and assaulted their self-esteem.

Fear, then, is the root cause of racism. And it can only be overcome by love. This is why I keep referring over and over again to Martin Luther King, Jr. This is why his dream is not dead. Whatever shortcomings he had as a human being, his enduring legacy is the vision of a single global family of humankind bound together by love. This is the revelation that was given to him when he went to the mountain top and saw the promised land. He might not have gotten there with us, but there was no doubt in his mind that we, as a people — all the children of God on planet earth — would get there some day. I mention Dr. King to appeal to the "better angels of our nature" in all of us. I do not intend to offend my white sisters and brothers by what I am contending about the nature of racism. I trust my words are a telling of the "truth in love," as St. Paul the apostle put it and in the spirit of that one after whom our son Jonathan is named. I can't help myself for being convinced that people in our society, especially white men and most specifically the "white male gerontocracy," because it is really they who are in control, need to acknowledge and deal with this fear that resides in the deepest part of themselves. Until they do, Dr. King's dream will never come true.

The time has come to say something about my closest friend at this period in my life, Lewis Rambo. Lew is a colleague of mine on the SFTS Faculty where he is Professor of Psychology and Religion. When I returned to San Anselmo in 1981, the two of us hit it off immediately and gravitated to each other. He had joined the Faculty several years before in 1978 after I had left for Chinatown in 1977. From the beginning some 12 years ago now, we opened up to each other with remarkable candor, and have continued to do so ever since. Also from the beginning, we got into the habit of having lunch together at least once a week. It is not uncommon, to this day, for us to have lunch together two and three times a week. We never run out of things to talk about because we tell each other everything. Everything. There's basically only one subject that's important to me that we don't discuss: basketball. Well, nothing's perfect.

I praise and thank God for my friendship with Lew. I am filled with three things at the thought of him: gratitude, humility, and hope. Along with members of Susan's immediate family, Lew is the one person who was present at the airport when Jonathan arrived from Korea on May 9, 1985 and Rebecca on June 26, 1987. Among his many talents is his skill as a photographer. He took wonderful pictures on those two original "chosen days" of our children. Perhaps the best thing about being adopted is that in addition to the day you came out of your biological mother's womb, you also get a second birthday every year. At any rate, I think the point is clear that Lew and I are the absolute best of friends. We were engaged in male bonding even before it was called that and before Billy Crystal's hit movie, *City Slickers*. This isn't to say we see everything eye to eye and are ideological clones. It occurs to me now to mention that Lew is of the Caucasian persuasion, which, of course, has no bearing on the content of his character, but was a major factor in an incident that took place between us.

We had been friends for perhaps a year at the time. We were as consciously honest with each other about every subject as I think it is possible for any two normally neurotic people to be. Some in San Anselmo might question the adverb "normally," but I don't think you'll get any argument with the adjective the adverb is modifying. Be that as it may, as time went on in that first year, Lew would make off-the-wall racial comments to me, in jest, both publicly and privately. They made me feel very uncomfortable. I'm sure every person of color with even a modicum of racial consciousness knows what I'm talking about. For the longest time, I overlooked them. Even though it bothered me, I was afraid to bring up the subject. I didn't want to risk hurting him or getting hurt myself. Finally, however, over one of our weekly lunches, he made one of those obnoxious comments—I can't remember exactly what he said—and I just erupted. I also can't remember exactly what I said in response except that I personally attacked him for his racism. He was stunned. I can still see the look on his face as I write this sentence. It was like I had stuck a knife in his heart. We got through the remainder of our lunch as quickly as possible and returned to work at the seminary. I thought I had blown it. I thought this was the end of our friendship because I had violated him so that he would never be able to trust me again. I had hurt him deeply, and the consequence of my losing my temper was losing him as a friend. I went home that night as devastated and depressed as I've ever been in my life over a personal confrontation with another individual. I was just glad that Susan was waiting for me when I got back to Hercules. To Lew's credit, because I didn't have the courage to take the initiative after what I'd done, he called me the very next morning in my office. We went out for lunch that same day. After sleeping on it, he proceeded to tell me, while munching on the world's greatest hamburger at Chez Phyllis on the miracle mile in San Rafael, once he got over the initial shock and attendant defensiveness, he was perplexed more than anything else. Man, was I relieved. I thought there was a chance he might not ever speak to me again, and here he was asking me for advice to overcome his racism. The rest, as they say, as far as our friendship is concerned, is history. As far as the racism point is concerned, even though he went to Yale, has a Ph.D. from the University of Chicago, has published a number of excellent books, and is perhaps the world's leading authority on the subject of conversion, because he was willing to let me be his teacher, he is one of the infinitesimally small percentage of those of the Caucasian persuasion, in my opinion, who has transcended racism. Like alcoholism, however, an alcoholic never stops being an alcoholic. One becomes a reformed alcoholic. In the same manner, white people never cease to be racists, but it is possible for them to become a reformed, and ever reforming, racist.

An issue I want to address now is the ripple effect the unconscious, deep-seated fear of black men has on the way the white male power structure treats individuals of other racial minority groups. Because Indians, Latinos, and Asians don't engender the same kind of primitive fear in white people, either in terms of sex or aggression, members of these three communities are chosen ahead of African Americans both as marriage partners and work colleagues. Protests to the contrary, if we are honest with ourselves, there can be no denying that this is true. Leaving aside the sex and marriage question, except to say the stigma is much greater for black-white couples than any of the other three combinations, when it comes to jobs, African Americans get the short end of the stick. Speaking as an Asian male, it troubles me when one of us is hired at the expense of a black sister or brother. I say this to minimize in no way, shape, or form the racism that those of us of brown, red, and yellow hue have had to endure and continue to suffer in terms of employment opportunities and professional advancement. The fact of the matter is, however, in my own personal experience, being an Asian American has worked more for me than against me. Especially in my current position which fills me with gratitude, humility, and hope, I would not be where I am today were I not a member of my particular racial minority group. The Presbyterian Church (USA) as a denomination and San Francisco Theological Seminary in particular have been most fair and generous to me. I wouldn't trade places job-wise with anyone in the world at this time in my life. I thank God for meaningful work to do and consider it a privilege and blessing to be what and where I am.

I have been very hard on the "white male gerontocracy." I have caricatured the members of this group as much as I have accused mass media of stereotyping Korean and African Americans in hackneyed ways. It is time to set the record straight. I do not hate them. I do not believe they are evil incarnate and beyond redemption. Martin Luther King, Jr. once said, "You can love people without liking them." In this spirit, I know in my heart I *love* them but do not *like* the things their policies do to us racial minority folks most of the time. Once in a while, the "old boys' club" does right by us. It is to one of these examples, involving one of its number that took place at the seminary not too long ago, that I now turn. The President of our school is a man named the Reverend Doctor J. Randolph Taylor. Randy, as everyone calls him, is a giant in our denomination. He is best known for having led the effort to reunite the two major streams of American Presbyterianism, north and south, which had divided in the previous century during Civil War times over the issue of slavery. In recognition of his work, he was elected Moderator in 1983 of the General Assembly of the newly merged Presbyterian Church (USA) that came into existence that year. A life-long Southerner, he became President of SFTS in 1985 and is retiring in June, 1994.

Randy and I have a good relationship. Early on in his tenure, I went to him privately to consult with him about the advisability of giving a paper that was sure to be very critical of both our denomination and SFTS for their racial justice track record. Like Jim Jones many years before, recalling the controversial Vietnam sermon I preached at Westminster Church as a young pastor fresh out of seminary, Randy said to me, "Warren, you can say anything you want as long as it's true." In that initial conversation, he shared with me some of his own personal experience with racial matters and mentioned the special influence Martin Luther King, Jr. had on him when he was a pastor in Atlanta, Georgia. From that time on, there has been a genuine bond between us two that I trust and celebrate. His wonderful wife Arlene is a big basketball fan. Being from North Carolina, she *loves* Michael Jordan. It touched me deeply that shortly after Magic Johnson's shocking announcement in the fall of 1991 that he had contracted the HIV virus and was retiring from the NBA, Randy telephoned me personally to check to see how I was doing. Needless to say, he is a pastor at heart. I'd bet my bottom dollar he is the only seminary president in America who did anything like that for one of his faculty members that sad day.

Through the years I have had a number of conversations with Randy about racial issues at the seminary. He knows that I have some problems with his leadership on this score when it comes to African Americans. To me it is ludicrous and unconscionable that Professor James Noel is the only black member on the Faculty, and that in the entire history of SFTS since our founding in 1871 we have never had more than one African American professor at any given time (with a grand total of three). Currently we have 4 Asian males, 1 black, no Hispanics, and no Native Americans. The numbers speak for themselves, and I want to make it clear that as an Asian I am not complaining because we are not an "under-represented constituency" at the seminary. Be that as it may, at a recent annual autumn Faculty retreat, Randy and I were participants in a small group discussion on strategic directions for the institution. Our group talked about the issue of inclusiveness and would later report our recommendations to the Faculty at a plenary session. We arrived at a consensus on a statement as follows: "Develop and implement a comprehensive affirmative action strategy to, with, and for African Americans at all levels of the seminary's life." I wrote this sentence down and gave it to Randy with the understanding he would read it verbatim at the plenary the next hour. To be sure, there were many items discussed and other concerns were put in writing and handed to him. When he reported the results of our small group conversation to the Faculty as a whole, he did not read my statement. I couldn't believe it. I was upset, angry, and then, outraged. Sinister thoughts entered my mind. I felt he had deliberately omitted what only a few minutes before he had asked me to write down. I concluded that "the devil made him do it," and it was a case of the demon racism having struck again. Rationally I thought to myself that as President he simply was unwilling to make this kind of institutional commitment to African Americans. The plenary was the last meeting of the afternoon so after it was over we adjourned for the day. Fortunately, I saw several fellow members of our small group and they felt the same way I did. I drove home across the Richmond-San Rafael Bridge and slept on it.

 Our annual autumn Faculty retreat is a two day affair so we met again first thing the following morning. As soon as I arrived before the opening session began, I saw Randy standing alone and asked him if we could talk for a few minutes. We found a quiet spot, and I proceeded to get the matter off my chest. I entered the conversation with some degree of fear and trepidation, but I told him I had to say what I was saying because until this point in our personal relationship from my end of things there was no emotional garbage polluting the atmosphere between us. I wanted to keep it that way, and not harbor resentment and hostility toward him as a person from then on. I let him have it with both barrels. Randy is not a defensive person to begin with, and he did not respond defensively at that time. He appeared genuinely perplexed, apologized, and said he appreciated my mentioning this to him. However, I thought the case was closed and that was that. A few minutes later the opening plenary session began. Randy asked for the floor and said something had just been brought to his attention that he needed to bring up to the Faculty. He then proceeded to explain what had happened and stated he needed to set the record straight. He read the sentence I had handed to him the previous afternoon. He declared unequivocally to the Faculty that he was committed 100% to the development and implementation of a comprehensive affirmative action strategy to, with, and for African Americans at every level of the seminary's life. All the members of our small group made eye contact and breathed a collective sigh of relief. I never felt better about a member of the "white male gerontocracy" than at that very moment. James Noel, who had also been in the small group, raised his hand. He told us that he hadn't slept very well the preceding night. He continued in his eloquent and powerful manner to say he was feeling good now. What the President had just done transformed his mood from doom to gloom, sorrow to joy, and darkness to light. God had surprised us once again when we least expected it. It was my turn next to testify to the glory and power of the Creator. I shared my feelings of gratitude, humility, and hope for what Randy, unprompted and on his own initiative, had the courage and vision to do. Someone then reminded us that the following day would be the 30th anniversary of the 1963 March on Washington. Martin Luther King's dream was never more alive and well than in that instant.

This brings me to the end of chapter 5. I want to close it with a final thought stated in the black idiom that I first heard in a sermon preached by Dr. King. It pertains not only to the descendants of slaves but applies to American society as a whole and to me personally: "We ain't what we wanna be, we ain't what we oughtta be, we ain't what we gonna be; but thank God we ain't what we was."

CHAPTER 6

# I Believe in the Resurrection

I have a good friend who lives and works in Houston, Texas named William Taegel. I met him during my first stint at SFTS in the mid 70's. He was a doctoral student at the time, and is now the head of a counseling agency where he is engaged in a thriving private practice. I have great admiration and deep affection for both him and his wife Judith, whose wedding I preformed in 1975. William attended the Candler School of Theology of Emory University in Atlanta, Georgia. He told me about an experience he had while a student there that is indelibly etched in my mind and heart. He was assigned to field work at the office of the Southern Christian Leadership Conference. The SCLC, of course, is the civil rights organization that originally grew out of the Montgomery bus boycott that had begun late in 1955 and was headed by Martin Luther King, Jr. My friend, albeit of the Caucasian persuasion, is no ordinary white dude. He is absolutely trustworthy, deeply sensitive about racial matters, knows when to speak up and when to keep his mouth shut, and perhaps most importantly of all, is blessed with common sense. As a result, he was taken into the inner circle of the SCLC and got to know a number of the key players in the Civil Rights Movement. Included were people like Jesse Jackson, Andrew Young, Ralph Abernathy, Hosea Williams, Dr. King himself, and Dr. King's father, the Rev. Martin Luther King, Sr. One day it happened that he was present at a strategy meeting of the top level leaders as they were in the middle of a major demonstration. It must be important to keep in mind that this was the early 60's, long before Memphis and 1968. The discussion was highly charged emotionally and feelings ran high as different opinions were expressed about how the SCLC should handle the situation and which individuals should assume what roles in the campaign at hand. Martin Luther King, Jr.

himself was not present at the meeting, but his father was. Tempers flared and in a heated exchange over the effectiveness of the non-violent method, suddenly, someone shouted at Daddy King, "What are you going to do when your son is assassinated?" Silence filled the room. After what seemed like an eternity, the elder and solemn Dr. King slowly rose to his feet. Looking straight into the eyes of the one who had yelled out the prophetic question, he said, "What am I going to do when my son is assassinated? I believe in the resurrection."

I, too, believe in the resurrection, as never before and with every fiber of my being. It undergirds my dream for South Central L.A. Given the kind of violent world and brutal society in which we live, it is finally the only reason I have any hope at all left in me. I recall what my second mother, Consuelo Adams, told me in that hospital room at Kaiser Permanente on Sunset Boulevard in 1980, when the doctors informed her that she would be gone within a month: "We may not know *what* the future holds, but we know *who* holds the future, even Jesus Christ our Lord." In the Preface to this book I said that I didn't have any simple or easy answer to the problem of the tensions between Korean and African Americans, and by extension, to the intractable dilemma of racism in our society. Well, it's true, I don't have a simple or easy answer, but I *do* have an answer: Jesus Christ, the same yesterday, today, and forever. I stand with Daddy King. I believe in the resurrection.

This resurrection faith in turn gives me the spiritual and emotional power to keep on keepin' on in the struggle against racism and all the other myriad forces of evil in our broken world. It creates the love which alone casts out the fear that is the root cause of what ails people in general and my own sin. Hatred and injustice born out of fear can be overcome. If I didn't believe that, I wouldn't have bothered to write this book. If it isn't true and if human beings really are incapable of change, we might as well all be dead. This applies to everyone regardless of color — white, black, brown, red, and yellow. What would be the point of going on? Albert Camus was right in *The Myth of Sisyphus* when he contended that there is only one ultimate philosophical question regarding the human predicament, the decision of whether or not to commit suicide. I choose not to kill myself, but for reasons different than those of the great French existentialist. I choose to continue the struggle, not by virtue of any noble heroism I can muster on my own in the face of life's inherent absurdity, I go on because of the gift of faith given to me by God to believe in Jesus Christ as Savior and Lord. The good news of the gospel tells me that crucifixion is not the final word about the meaning of human existence. If it were, the obnoxious bumper sticker I see all too often while driving across the Richmond-San Rafael Bridge would be only all too true, "Life is rough and then you die." Life *is* rough. And then we *do* die. But, thank you, Jesus, we live again. The cross has power to heal, not because Jesus was killed on one. The cross has the power to redeem because it convicts us of the infinitely greater truth that three days later He rose again from the dead. Good Friday is only "good" because it was followed by Easter morning.

When Daddy King testified to the reality of his Christian faith by retorting, "I believe in the resurrecton," he had no idea that in a few years his son would be awarded the Nobel Peace Prize, a few years after that, he would be shot and killed outside a Memphis, Tennessee motel, and two and a half decades after that, the United States Government would create a national holiday to commemorate his birthday. No, I'm sure, when Daddy King said what he did, he was speaking as just that, a daddy. If he had a choice, no doubt he would have traded all the acclaim and notoriety that came his son's way, notwithstanding his child's place in history and what he accomplished for posterity, for his having not "gone too soon." Dr. King was only 39 years old when James Earl Ray zeroed in on his head with a high-powered rifle and pulled the trigger. I am convinced that the single greatest loss in human life is the death of a child to a parent. It reverses the order of things. It doesn't make sense. It is impossible to accept psychologically. I am never surprised to hear that a mom or dad, or both, have committed suicide after their daughter or son has died, especially if the victim had been an only child. If there are other kids in the family, parents will go on for their sake but not the parents' own.

This is why I'm glad I'm a Christian, and plan on continuing to be one. Christian faith speaks directly to the deepest anguish of the human condition. In our times of greatest sorrow and loss, it presents us with news too good to be true. Nothing we can do will lessen the immediate sense of heartache we feel and it may linger for many seasons, but there can be no doubt as to the final outcome. God knows the place we are in when our children are taken away from us too soon. God knows, because She was in the same place when Her own Son was killed. I am reminded of an interview I saw on television some years ago with Rose Kennedy. She was then in her late 80's but as beautiful, bright, warm, and charming as ever. The interviewer was very skilled and asked questions on a wide variety of subjects. Mrs. Kennedy shared a lot of personal information about her relationship with her late husband and told many interesting stories about her 9 children. Inevitably, as the interview was coming to an end, the subject of all the suffering she has had to endure in her lifetime came up — the death of 4 children, 3 sons and a daughter, the fact of her institutionalized developmentally disabled daughter, and her feelings regarding the assassinations of President John Kennedy and Senator Robert Kennedy. Even though it was obviously very painful for her to share her recollections and reflections about these sad and tragic events, she did so with great honesty, dignity, and understanding. She expressed no trace of bitterness when asked about Lee Harvey Oswald and Sirhan Sirhan. At one point, she smiled and related the story about how all her friends urged her not to have her ninth and last child, Teddy, and how if she would have listened to their well intentioned advice and done the sensible thing, i.e., abortion, she would then have had no sons at all. Finally, the interviewer asked this great and wonderful American woman, "Mrs. Kennedy, how did you get through all of this? What is it about you that you have been able to survive these unspeakably heartbreaking tragedies and not become bitter and cynical, much less gone mad from the pain and anguish?" As her eyes glistened, she replied, "My greatest comfort and source of strength has been my faith in God. I have often thought of how the Holy Mother must have felt as she saw her son dying on the cross that dark Friday afternoon so many years ago."

    I have already quoted the late, great James Baldwin employing the phrase "the fire next time." It was the title of a book he wrote in 1963 and the refrain was used over and over again in commentaries on the spring, 1992 Los Angeles upheavals. I want to quote him now in a different context. It reflects the state of both soul and mind he had come to near the end of his life, and is similar to the point where Malcolm X had arrived before his premature death by assassination in 1965. By the way, the person who told me about this line is none other than the Breeze, my brother in the Faith and protege on the hardwood. Michael saw James Baldwin on television being interviewed shortly before he died. The outspoken and controversial literary genius was asked what he would like his final message to the world to be. He replied, "What we all need to do is, raise our children and love each other." Period. If we do this, there will be no "fire next time." He didn't say *that*, but I just did. When I was a student at UCLA, I once attended a lecture that James Baldwin gave. I came away from it realizing the media was wrong to portray him as they did. He may have been angry because of racial injustice, but even then he exuded love and spoke of the need for reconciliation and healing. He wasn't filled with hate toward white people. He seemed to like everybody and certainly the overwhelmingly Caucasian audience responded to him with openness and warmth. I especially enjoyed the question and answer period following his formal presentation. It needs to be kept in mind that this was the early 60's when the Civil Rights Movement was peaking. The eminent author was asked to comment on all the major black leaders of the day. He had interesting insights and unique angles on everyone. Finally, a questioner asked him about Martin Luther King, Jr. A big smile came to his wonderfully expressive face with those huge, bulging eyes and he replied, "What you always have to remember about Martin is, he's a Christian. I mean, he *really* is."

I will never forget January 28, 1986. I had awakened early in the morning to watch the launch of the Challenger on television from Cape Canaveral. I was particularly excited because for the first time in history an African American, Ron McNair, and an Asian American, Ellison Onizuka, were going up in space. The lion's share of the publicity, understandably so, had gone to Christa McAuliffe, a school teacher from New England who was not an astronaut. She would be the first private citizen to orbit the earth as a result of having been selected by NASA in a highly competitive nation-wide recruitment campaign. This was all well and good with me, but my special joy in the impending flight was due to the fact that two people of color were set to go. My excitement grew as the countdown began. The engines were ignited, "Five-four-three-two-one, ladies and gentlemen, we have a lift-off." My heart soared as I watched that big white bird fly straight up higher and higher into the sky. The Jonathan Livingson Seagull in me was soaring too. The camera followed the aircraft on its upward flight when suddenly it broke up into two pieces like a giant wishbone. At first, I said to myself, "Wow! What a spectacular sight." For an instant, I thought it was planned that way and everything was okay. As I continued to watch, however, and saw the faces of the McAuliffe family turn from sublime joy, to confusion, to fear, to horror, I knew something drastically wrong had happened. Although not identical, the devastation I felt was similar in tone to the assassinations of President John Kennedy, Dr. Martin Luther King, Jr., and Senator Robert Kennedy. I will always remember what I was doing on January 28, 1986.

My thoughts turned immediately to the families of the seven crew members of the Challenger who had just seen what I had seen. At this point, I was still hoping against hope that they had somehow managed to survive the steep descent back to the surface of the earth. After all, the space capsule had splashed down into the waters of the Atlantic Ocean. My mind told me that my heart was foolish to think this way, but I kept saying to myself, "It's true, with human beings it's not possible, but with God all things are possible. Dear God, please God, please let them be alright. Make this nightmare go away." When it became clear that they had all perished in the flight, I was disconsolate. I was in a state of shock. The depression and despair I felt were utter and complete. All the aspirations and dreams of a lifetime for many people, and the blood, sweat, and tears of thousands of others, plus the hopes of tens of millions more watching in their living rooms, had gone up instantaneously in a plume of smoke. It goes without saying that life can be capricious and unbearably cruel at times. It seems totally unfair. Upon more careful reflection, however, I think there's a deeper and even more painful reality operating here. It is captured in a terse aphorism delivered in a television mini-series I saw some years ago entitled *The Last Cadillac*. As trashy as the program sounds and was, the following one-liner stuck with me because of its compelling truth:

"Life *is* fair. It breaks everybody's heart." I recall a sermon I once heard by an old black preacher as he was waxing eloquent on the subject of the problem of evil: "So you think what I'm preaching about this morning has no relevance to you because you or no loved one of yours has suffered. I have only one word to say to you: wait."

And so it was, I found myself waiting in front of the T.V. sinking further and further into the abyss. Then, as instantly and unexpectedly as the accident itself, in the twinkling of an eye, Daddy King's words came to me. "I believe in the resurrection." This conviction, and this alone, provided me the consolation I needed to see me through the tragedy I had just witnessed. The only comfort I had after the Challenger went down was the doctrine of the resurrection. Accordingly and finally, it is my sole consolation in the face of death itself. My faith tells me Ron McNair, Ellison Onizuka, Christa McAuliffe and the four other astronauts who lost their lives in that ill-fated flight did not die in vain. Their family and loved ones may never know why they were taken away from them so suddenly and arbitrarily. Whatever the reason, discovering it won't bring them back. To those who were left behind, there is only one message that matters. What I want to tell them is that when they waved goodbye on the launch pad on the morning of January 28, 1986 is not the last time they'll see each other again. Sure, it was the last time as far as this world is concerned. But, to answer with the promise of the gospel another cynical sentiment of the bumper sticker variety, "Is That All There Is?" I am here to testify that no, this is not all there is. Jesus said, "I am the resurrection and the life. They who believe in me, though they were dead, yet shall they live: whoever lives and believes in me shall never die." I have already made it plain to my dear wife Susan that at my funeral I want the Reverend Professor Marsha Foster Boyd of United Theological Seminary in Dayton, Ohio to sing, "I know my redeemer liveth and that He shall stand at the latter day. Though worms destroy this body, yet will I see God in the flesh." Speaking now as a Presbyterian minister, I offer to the bereaved from the space shuttle disaster and the disconsolate where'er ye languish, the following words from one of the great confessions of our particular theological tradition, the *Heidelberg Catechism* (Question 1. and Answer): "Q.1. What is your only comfort in life and death? A. That I belong body and soul, in life and in death—not to myself but to my faithful Saviour, Jesus Christ, who at the cost of his own blood has fully paid for all sins and has completely freed me from the dominion of the devil; that he protects me so well that without the will of my Father in heaven not a hair can fall from my head; indeed, that everything must fit his purpose for my salvation. Therefore, by his Holy Spirit, he also assures me of eternal life, and makes me wholeheartedly willing and ready from now on to live for him."

At this stage in my autobiographical journey and theological pilgrimage of faith, in addition to the doctrine of predestination and resurrection, it is the doctrine of forgiveness that has come to mean so much to me. Along with Lew Rambo, Dr. Jana Childers, our homiletics and speech professor at SFTS and acting Dean for the fall semester of 1993, is as close a personal friend I have at the seminary. She attended Wheaton College for her undergraduate degree and knows as many old gospel songs as I do. She is one of the greatest preachers I have ever heard in my life and is a ravishingly beautiful woman. In an Advent sermon she preached at a chapel service last year, the title of her message was "The Gift Worth Waiting For." In her customary fashion, she developed the subject brilliantly and built up to a perfect climax. Christmas has become so commercialized in our hedonistic and consumer-oriented society, it is difficult not to think in materialistic terms at this time of year — even for seminary professors and divinity students. "What is the gift worth waiting for?" asked the Reverend Professor Childers. "Forgiveness," she replied. Not a new car, not a new house, not a new anything, but a chance for a new life. Forgiveness is indeed the gift worth waiting for at Christmas, and it is available every other day of the year.

The starting place for Korean and African Americans to resolve the tensions between them is forgiveness. It's true, as well, for whites and blacks, gays and straights, women and men, husbands and wives, parents and children, Arabs and Jews, Serbs and Croats. Name any broken relationship, and forgiveness works every time. Trust me. Try it, you'll like it. I realize it is very easy to say this in the abstract and probably no one would disagree with the point. I do not mean to trivialize the evil we human beings perpetrate on each other, both as individuals and groups. Furthermore, the Christian doctrine of forgiveness is not a matter of what the great German theologian, Dietrich Bonhoeffer, who was executed by the Nazis for participating in a plot to assassinate Adolf Hitler, called "cheap grace." Among his many influential writings is a book entitled *The Cost of Discipleship* (New York: Macmillan, 1963) where he discussed this notion. Being a Christian doesn't make forgiveness easy, it makes it hard. Why? Because our faith requires not only compassion for the sinner who committed the wrong, but love for the victim and needs to include ourselves if we were the one that was wronged. In this spirit, then, acknowledging the cost and difficulty involved in forgiving evildoers in general and our personal enemies in particular, I want to share the following pair of illustrations, one about an African American and the other about a Korean.

First, believe it or not, is an encounter I had with Eldridge Cleaver. For those who might not have heard of him, he is the controversial man who initially came into the public eye in the late 60's. At that time he was the Minister of Information for the Black Panther Party and was once a candidate for the Presidency of the United States on the Peace and Freedom Party ticket. He wrote a brilliant book while he was in prison, *Soul on Ice* (New York: Delta Books, 1968), his spiritual and intellectual autobiography, which was widely read and highly acclaimed in those turbulent days. He eventually fled the country to escape imprisonment again and lived for several years in exile in Algeria. He even visited North Korea during that period, where his wife Kathleen gave birth to a child. He returned voluntarily to America in 1976 and was incarcerated in Oakland, California amid great publicity and fanfare. It was announced that he had become a "born again" Christian, and it was this decision more than anything else which led him to come back home. In subsequent years, he did things which changed his public image completely. He became an entrepeneur and opened a line of men's clothing. He also ran unsuccessfully for Mayor of the City of Oakland. I think it's safe to say that he was portrayed in the media as a "flake," and is regarded as one now by the majority of people who have followed his career from the beginning and would still recognize his name today. To be sure, he no

95

longer strikes terror in the hearts of white people, anymore than, say, Angela Davis. After the hoopla which surrounded her in this same period faded away, she has been living quietly in the San Francisco Bay Area for over 20 years utilizing her considerable intellectual gifts as a college professor. I don't believe Angela ever did want to "die nobly for a cause." She was always willing to "live humbly for one." Media racism simply wouldn't let her be the kind and gentle human being she was all along that the test of time has proven to be so.

It was perhaps a decade ago that I spotted Eldridge Cleaver boarding the same plane I was taking to return home to San Francisco from Philadelphia. David Connolly had just dropped me off at the airport, and I was feeling melancholy as I usually do after one of our always all-too-short visits. I don't think very many, if any, of the passengers on the flight, overwhelmingly white, recognized this once infamous and notorious former Black Panther. Besides, all colored folks, including we Asians, "look alike" to them. As the case may be, *I* knew who he was and felt the urge to introduce myself to him. I resisted this temptation, however, figuring there's no reason he would want to talk to me. I took my seat on the plane and settled in for the long 5 ½ hour trip. Since there's always a movie to watch on transcontinental flights, I rented a headset. After we were served our meal, the movie was turned on. It stopped less than a minute later. There was some mechanical glitch and we would not be able to see the film. To me, this was a sign from God. Her still small voice then whispered in my ear, "Breeze, don't be such a wimp. Just go up to Eldridge Cleaver and ask if it's okay to talk." "Yes, Mommie dearest," I replied, and walked over to Mr. Soul on Ice. Naturally, there were two vacant seats next to him because the Creator had written my name on them. For the next 4 ½ hours we jawed non-stop on every subject known to humankind.

One reason I was fairly certain he wouldn't mind having a conversation with me, if only he would agree to give me a few minutes, is that there was one person I knew we had in common. Her name is Judy Graham. Her parents attended worship at the Westminster Presbyterian Church in L.A. from time to time when I was there from 1966 to 1973. I would always find some excuse to pay a pastoral call on the Grahams because Judy might be there and she was as fine as wine. She looked like a cross between Marilyn McCoo and Robin Givens. My knees grew weak and my palms began to sweat every time I was in her presence. Weak knees, sweaty palms, and my gone-with-the-breeze fantasies aside, Judy eventually married a man named Emory Douglas. He had replaced Eldridge Cleaver as the Minister of Information of the Black Panther Party. The two of them, Emory and Judy, had made a secret six week trip to Algeria to visit the Cleavers when they were in exile there. Judy told me that her husband's predecessor was the "nicest, kindest, gentlest, and most wonderful man" she had ever met in her life. This, of course, was completely contrary to his media image at the time. When I told Eldridge how Judy had described him to me, whatever defensiveness he might have felt initially, melted away. We really did talk about everything. I was very interested, for example, in his experience in North Korea. The most striking thing I remember about this is a group he mentioned called something like the "Young Men's Red Brigade." The name's not important but their reason for being blew my mind. In order to become a member, it was necessary to vow not to have sexual relations until Korea was reunited. "My God," I said to myself, "these kimchee-eating cousins in my ancestral homeland are some serious dudes!"

    Be that as it may, in view of the notoriety that surrounded Eldridge's return from exile in 1976, bail in the Oakland courtroom where he was arraigned was set at an inordinately high amount, $100,000. He told me he was concerned for his life at that point and would not have been surprised had an attempt to assassinate him been made while he was in custody. However, he had taken this danger into consideration in his decision to turn himself in and was fully aware of the danger involved. Having become a born again Christian, the doctrine of the resurrection had come to mean the same thing for him as it does to me. It was his encounter with Jesus Christ as a living reality that brought him home in the first place. He had made no deals with anyone. He had decided completely on his own, save his wife Kathleen's opinions, to take this leap of faith into the unknown. As he was waiting in jail, uncertain of whether or not he would be killed at any moment, he received a letter from a wealthy Christian layman from

Valley Forge, Pennsylvania named Arthur De Moss. He said that he had just come across an article in the *Los Angeles Times* about Eldridge's situation and was deeply impressed by the courage it took to do what he had done. As a born again Christian himself, he had found it in his heart to forgive the now redeemed Black Panther for all his past sins. In closing he personally guaranteed to put up $100,000. I am not trying to defend Eldridge Cleaver and make any special claim to know who he really is or isn't. In the words of the old Johnny Mathis ballad, "It's not for me to say." I do believe, however, that in the providence of God, our 4 ½ hour conversation did not happen by chance. In being filled with gratitude, humility, and hope for the experience, I know that it was predestined to take place and meant to appear in this book.

The second illustration I want to share is an incident about a Korean Presbyterian minister named the Reverend Doctor Han, Kyung Chik. He is perhaps the single most revered and well known Korean Christian in the world today, at least to us Korean people ourselves. Now 92 years old, he is regarded as a kind of national religious treasure and living Protestant saint. He founded the Young Nak Presbyterian Church in Seoul in 1946, and the current membership is approximately 60,000. Yes, you heard right, 60 *thousand*, and they all go to church every Sunday. I know, I've been there many times. In 1991 he received the Templeton Prize, an award similar to the various Nobel prizes given annually in the field of religion. Past recipients include people like the Dalai Lama, Mother Teresa, and Billy Graham. It is the single largest monetary award of its kind, worth in excess of a million dollars. Upon receiving it in the official ceremony in Berlin, Dr. Han promptly announced he was donating the money to help rebuild Christian churches in North Korea. The reason it was North Korea is that this is where he was born and from where he had fled after the Communists took control following World War II. My father, who died at the age of 86 in 1984, and Dr. Han had been classmates at Soong Sil University in Pyong Yang, the first Christian college in Korea, in the second decade of this century. I have known him all my life and he is like a second father to me.

An incident occurred not long after he had returned home to Korea after receiving the Templeton Prize in 1991. A grand welcoming home banquet was held in his honor sponsored by the Young Nak Church. If ever there was a moment for a human being to bask in glory and enjoy the adulation of the crowd, this was it. After the meal was eaten and all the congratulatory speeches were made, when it was his turn to speak, Dr. Han did something that truly sets him apart from other people. This wonderful and holy man asked for forgiveness. In hushed silence, he told those gathered to honor him that he had been carrying a deep wound and burden in his soul that he had kept secret for almost 60 years. I'm sure he did not consciously intend to make this announcement when the evening began, it simply came out spontaneously.

In 1935 the Imperial Japanese colonial government in Korea began a policy requiring student and government employee attendance at Shinto ceremonies. Many Christians closed their schools and churches rather than accede to the order. A number of foreign missionaries were expelled and several thousand ministers were arrested between 1935 and 1938. Some pastors even courageously chose to die as martyrs during this period. Dr. Han confessed that he had always harbored a deep sense of guilt about not actively resisting this forced Shinto-shrine policy which resulted in the arrest and even death of so many of his Christian friends and fellow pastors. At long last he was bringing this hidden sorrow out into the open. What an extraordinary time and place to make such a revelation! What an act of sacrifice and courage! Only a true saint could be capable of this kind of utter vulnerability and naked humility. This is why Dr. Han, Kyung Chik is a Christian for *all* ages—the highest, purest, and best example of following in the footsteps of Jesus Christ our living Lord and Savior… " who did not consider equality with God a thing to be grasped but emptied himself taking upon himself the form of a servant." Forgiveness lies at the very heart of the gospel. Jana Childers was right. It is the greatest gift anyone can ever give or receive, and it is always the one worth waiting for 365 days of the year.

There is another Korean Presbyterian minister I want to discuss now. I have mentioned him several times in passing already but the time has come to say more about him in depth. His name is the Reverend Doctor Shungnak Luke Kim. He served as the Pastor of the

Korean Presbyterian Church in Los Angeles, where I grew up, from 1938 to 1959. He baptized me as an infant, as well as my sisters Sally and June, and performed Susan's and my wedding as well as my sister Kay's and her husband Wayne. His son George is the one I talked about in "Lust Is Blond" who had attended Wooster College in Ohio where he was a star basketball player and B.M.O.C. Kimbo, as he is called, and I were the backcourt tandem on the Korean Presbyterian Church team that took back-to-back All-City Church Athletic Association of Los Angeles championship titles in 1962-63. Dr. Kim was born and raised in Pyong Yang. An alumnus of Soong Sil University, he returned to Korea in 1959 to become its President. In the 1920's he attended Yale University Divinity School and Princeton Theological Seminary, and earned both a Th.D. and Ph.D. degree. As pastor of our small ethnic church in South Central L.A. for 21 years, he never earned more than $1300 annually. His wife, the same as my mother and many other Korean immigrant women, worked in a downtown Los Angeles sewing factory, earning and saving money to raise their six children.

Dr. Kim was perhaps the single most highly educated person I have ever known. He was an accomplished scholar and brilliant intellectual. He was also universally recognized as the symbolic leader of the First Wave Korean American community in Los Angeles. When I look back at the meaning of his life and ministry for me now, I realize that what I learned most from him is the lesson of humility. Wealth, power, status, and success were not important values to him. He was first and foremost a pastor, whose greatest ability was to love and care for people. I saw him cry at many funerals including my sister Aikyung's in 1968. I officiated at Dr. Kim's funeral in Los Angeles in 1989 when he died at the age of 86. I cried.

There's a story I want to share now that Dr. Kim told me about which originates from his graduate school days in the mid 1920's at Yale University in New Haven, Connecticut. He met and became friends with a student from Japan there. Because of colonialism, Dr. Kim spoke fluent Japanese so they could communicate well with each other. Their common commitment to Jesus Christ enabled them in a relationship of two people to transcend the enmity which existed between their respective countries. Dr. Kim did not hold it against this individual for the untold evil that was being perpetrated on the Korean people and the personal indignities he had endured at the hands of Japan as a nation. This point, incidentally, should always be kept in mind when countries have disagreements and even go to war. We cannot blame the people of whatever nation is involved for the actions of its government. I may have hated Sadam Hussein during the Persian Gulf War, but I never allowed this sentiment to extend to the Iraqi people. The individual inhabitants of that historic and great land, home of the world's oldest civilization, were never my enemies. Dr. Kim and the Japanese young man, whom I shall call Toshio, became close friends in the context of the International Students Association at Yale. They parted company after a few years in New Haven never expecting to see each other again.

After finishing his education in America, Dr. Kim returned to Pyong Yang and became a minister in a church. He was pastoring a congregation there in 1935 when that same policy of the Imperial Japanese government, which I mentioned earlier in speaking about Dr. Han, was promulgated, forcing Koreans to attend Shinto ceremonies. From that time on, Christians suffered more greatly than any other group in the society because of their resistance to this edict. They were under constant surveillance and in many cases brutally harassed. In 1938 a secret order was given by the hated colonial police force to arrest a number of key Christian ministers for interrogation and possible imprisonment. Dr. Kim's name was on that list. It just so happened that Toshio had been assigned a position in the occupational government and had recently moved to Korea. Again, it just so happened that he and his old Yale Divinity School classmate ran into each other on a crowded bus in the heart of the city of Pyong Yang. Of course, they were completely surprised to see each other and had a joyous reunion. Several days later Dr. Kim received a clandestine telephone call in the middle of the night from Toshio telling him that he would be arrested soon. Toshio had made arrangements for him and his family to leave Pyong Yang immediately for the United States. This is the reason this wonderful and godly man came to America in 1938 to begin his ministry as Pastor of the Korean Presbyterian Church of Los Angeles.

This story leads me now to reveal my dream for South Central. Rooted in the gospel of Jesus Christ, it is neither a sociological or political answer to the tensions existing between blacks and Koreans. Nor does it speak to the social and economic ills which plague Los Angeles and urban America as a whole. I leave it to others with far greater expertise in these areas than myself to recommend the institutional steps which need to be taken in order to prevent the "fire next time." No, I speak as a preacher and a pastor. My message is a spiritual and theological one. I say, all of us—red, yellow, black, brown, and white—have a choice to make here. Either we're part of the problem, or we're part of the solution. Accordingly and specifically, for Korean and African Americans, my solution to the problem of the tensions between us, after the manner of Dr. Kim and Toshio, is for one person of each warring group to "reach out and touch" one person of the other group. However, this effort needs to be self-conscious and intentional. It cannot be casual and left to chance. It will require a certain amount of commitment and discipline because the fundamental pattern of our social activities is governed by racism. But, in the spirit of James Baldwin, whose parting words to us were to "raise our children and love each other," we can do it. If every single black person and every single Korean person in Los Angeles were to develop a personal relationship with an individual member of the other group in which love casts out fear, where genuine friendship such as I've taken great pains to describe throughout this book blossoms forth into reality in our two communities, I believe our problem can be solved. Very few of us can do much about poverty, unemployment, drugs, crime, police brutality, and domestic violence in general. There isn't a one of us who can't make a concerted effort to become a close friend of a single fellow human being of a different race from ourselves. This, then, in a nutshell, is my dream for South Central. Try it, you'll like it. And it'll work if you give it a chance. I promise.

The gospel of Jesus Christ tells me that a grain of mustard seed sown in faith will become the biggest shrub of all. The gospel of Jesus Christ tells me that giving up five loaves and two fishes can feed the whole multitude if we are willing to sacrifice what little we have for the good of the whole. Nancy Reagan admonished our young people to

"Just say no" to drugs. My plea is to "Just say yes" to each other. For us Koreans, say yes to black folks and get to know a Mother Flora A. Wright and Brother Freeman B. Gates. You will be healed emotionally and redeemed spiritually if you do. For African Americans, say yes to Korean folks and get to know a Shungnak Luke Kim and Kyung Chik Han, the same thing will happen to you. I have tried to say in these pages that Dr. King's dream is not dead and that "we shall overcome some day." I, too, like him, believe I've been to the mountain top and seen the promised land. I, too, may not get there, but I know that we, as a people — the whole family of humankind — will get there in the end. After all that's said and done, there is so much more that unites us than divides us. "In Christ there is no east or west, in Him no south or north. But one great fellowship of love throughout the whole wide earth." "Who shall separate us from the love of Christ? Shall famine, or nakedness, or peril, or sword? Nay, in all these things we are more than conquerors through Him that loved us. For I am persuaded, that neither death, nor life, nor angels, nor principalities, nor powers, nor things present, nor things to come, nor height, nor depth, nor any other creature, shall be able to separate us from the love of God, which is in Christ Jesus our Lord."

# EPILOGUE

The Lee family of Susan, Warren, Jonathan, and Rebecca make three or four automobile trips to Los Angeles from our home in Hercules every year. It's about 400 miles and takes around seven hours. The fuel gauge on our 1988 Plymouth Voyager mini-van has a mind of its own. Last year when driving down Interstate 5 just before the Grapevine, we came within an eye lash of running out of gas. On that same trip returning home, eight miles short of our destination, we did. Susan was upset enough about what *almost* happened on the way down, so when the car came chugging down to a stop, as we barely made it to a freeway off-ramp, she was ready to kill me. I mean, KILL.

We were in the city of Martinez in east Contra Costa County, about a mile from that "Republican Party in prayer" suburban church Mr. Ostrowski made sure — thank you, Jesus — I didn't get eleven years earlier. I mention this because the area where our mini-van ran out of gas is 99 and $^{44}/_{100}$% white. With Susan ready to commit an act of unspeakable violence on her spouse-fearing husband, and Jon and Rebe trembling at the prospect of never seeing their father in one piece again, I jumped out of the car as quickly as I could and made a mad dash for help. I ran about a quarter of a mile and found a shopping center. It was Sunday evening and the sun had already gone down so there weren't a lot of people around. I spotted someone coming out of a drug store and high-tailed it over to him. He was kind enough to hear me out and said not to worry. He had a gas can in the trunk of his car for just this reason. We walked a short distance to where it was parked, got in, and drove to the nearest service station. I filled the can and we went back to the off-ramp to find Susan and the kids waiting for us. Emptying the container into the tank of the Voyager, I introduced this wonderful man, who had saved my life, to the family. At about this time, I noticed this guy was black, in his late 20's or early 30's. He was dressed very casually and even looked a little like Rodney King. He told me he lived close by in the vicinity. I wonder how many times the cops have stopped him late at night in the city of Martinez. I thanked him profusely and even offered him some money, which he refused to take. I wanted to kiss him as we said goodbye. I can't even remember the man's name now although I recall asking him where he was from originally. "Detroit," he said, and naturally I told him how much I disliked the Pistons for beating the Lakers four straight in the 1989 NBA Finals to keep my team from three-peating. Of course, he thought Bill Laimbeer hadn't fouled Kareem Abdul-Jabbar the previous year when the greatest player in the history of the game sank those two crucial free throws in game 6 to force a seventh game, which, as everyone knows, the Lakers won to become the first team in 19 years to win back to back world championships.

On the short drive to Hercules, with calm having been restored, a now smiling Susan said, "It's been this way all your life, hasn't it, Breeze? Some African American always bails you out." "Yes, dear," I said, "ever since the second grade when Carmelita Brown and Melvin Johnson started watching out for me. It happens every time. Some sister or brother rescues me from harm even in the unlikeliest places." I believe if Jesus were to come back today, we would not recognize Him. He would meet us when we least expect Him, and we would be surprised by the way He looks and how He acts. After all, this is what happened the first time around. May we be granted eyes to see, ears to hear, and a heart to feel the Messiah who is never far from us and is always in our midst. Black folks have been angels of mercy and channels of love through which I have experienced the grace of God my entire life. I realize now it was all a part of the Creator's divine master plan and meant to be. And it ain't over yet. My heart continues to overflow with gratitude, humility, and hope. I know who that brother from Detroit was. Thank you, Jesus, and Amen.

BX
9225
.L44
A3
1993